The ___

Agile

Marketing

A Practical Roadmap for Implementing Kanban and
Scrum in Jira and Confluence

Outer Limits Media

BILL CUSHARD

The Art of Agile Marketing: A Practical Roadmap for Implementing Kanban and Scrum in Jira and Confluence by Bill Cushard. Published by Outer Limits Media P.O. Box 61235 Cambridge 265 Avenue, Palo Alto, CA 94306.

© 2018 Bill Cushard

Visit the author's website: billcushard.com

Cover by Bill Cushard

ISBN: 978-1-7324626-0-1

CONTENTS

Dedication

I'd like to dedicate this book to three people.

To Matt Doar, Engineer at Linkedin, who helped me set up my first kanban board way back in the olden days of 2013.

To Mark Gopez for letting Colleen Blake and I sit in on one of his marketing team's sprint retrospective meetings. Mark was generous with his time, and he opened our eyes to what a high performing, agile marketing team could look like.

To my wife, Kim, who told me to wake up and write. Sometimes she even told me to get some sleep.

Part One: Why Scrum

Introduction

"Make people better at something they want to be better at."
~ Kathy Sierra, Author
Badass: Making Users Awesome

So many books begin by saying the world is moving faster than ever before. Forces like globalization, mobile, social, cloud, SaaS, big data, IoT, VUCA, AI, AR, VR, machine learning, continuous development, continuous integration, DevOps, B.L.A.H., etc. Statements like this are not exactly helpful. First of all, they are too vague to be helpful. Second, no one seems to offer any evidence that it is true by any objective definition. It seems to me that time moves at the same speed as it ever did, so things actually are not speeding up. So, how could the world be moving faster than ever before?

Here's the truth. You are running around the office like a chicken with its head cut off, worrying about all the things you have to do. You have 27 things on your to-do list today and only time to do four of them. I am fairly confident that you are not worrying about IoT while you are trying to figure out your next marketing campaign, unless you work for Cisco or GE and you are selling a refrigerator that automatically orders more hummus when it detects you are down to your last four servings.

My bet is that you are worried about the 27 things on your list, how to pick the right four tasks to work on, and how to deal with the urgent requests that constantly add to your list.

The problem lies in the ongoing, endless, and rapidly accelerating growth of our to-do lists. It keeps coming at us, and it comes at us from all directions.

Just making decisions on what to work on is almost overwhelming and debilitating in and of itself. How many times have you sat at your desk and asked yourself out loud, "What should I work on next?" I ask myself that question every day.

This is a problem for two reasons.

First, it causes stress. Every day we sit at our desks and think about the hundreds of things we could work on and wonder, "What do I work on next? Is it the right thing to work on? I don't really know. Oh, look. Someone just sent me a notification on Workplace by Facebook with a request. I'll work on that." To make this decision easier, we often use our inboxes and messages as our to-do lists. This is not a good long-term strategy, but it helps us remain relevant to our stakeholders.

Even if we have SMART goals, OKRs, KPIs, rocks, or whatever we call them, it can be difficult to decide what to work on next. There is just too much coming at us. Goals are no match for the constant barrage of ideas, requests, and fires we deal with every day. Consider this "short" list:

- That social media engagement report
- That customer risk
- That escalation
- That emergency board meeting
- Your best marketing manager just quit

- The brochure for that event is due at the printer by noon today

Maybe some of you have it all together. I, for one, struggle with this every day. I want to do a good job. I want to help customers, increase the pipeline, help the sales team close more deals in less time, and create a work environment in which people can thrive. I want to create marketing that is useful and effective. My intentions are right, but I find myself sitting at my desk wasting a lot of time thinking about what to work on next without a clear method for deciding what to do next. Standing in the way of my good intentions is the constant flow of things I could work on.

That is stressful.

What if I pick the wrong thing? What if I pick five things, they are all the right things, but I am spread so thin, I cannot deliver well on any of them? Is it better to ignore four out of five important things and do one exceptionally well? Or pick three of the five and do those fairly well?

Working stressfully is not sustainable. It leads to burnout, low performance, and chronic fatigue.

For us to be successful; for us to work in an environment that minimizes stress, we need to develop competence in evaluating these requests in the context of our ultimate goal (or big picture) and decide if we should focus on it or not. I wrote this book to help you develop that competence.

Second, the act of choosing what to work on next prevents us from maximizing our contribution to our organizations and to our work.

In addition to causing stress, this constant barrage of information is holding us back from being at our best.

The most important thing marketers should do is understand the growth goals of our business and work backwards to develop marketing that is specifically designed to help the organization achieve those growth goals. Then, execute that plan.

Nothing else matters.

We know this. And yet, we struggle to do it as effectively as we would like.

Why?

Because we spread ourselves so thin, that we do not focus on the fewest, most important projects and tasks that would make the most important contribution to the company. Because in the moment, everything seems important.

But everything is not important. In his book, *The Effective Executive: The Definitive Guide to Getting the Right Things Done*, Peter F. Drucker argues that "executives are paid for effectiveness." Not hard work. Effectiveness. "Intelligence, imagination, and knowledge are essential resources," says Drucker, "but only effectiveness converts them into results." Effectiveness, therefore, is the art of converting our "smarts" into results.

Except, requests just keep coming at us, from all directions. There might be two requests from product, three from the CEO, four from customers, two from that last report, three from sales, one from the CFO. And that is all from this morning alone. To the requesters, they are not asking for a lot. But to you, you are now dealing with 15 requests, and you cannot handle them all.

Am I supposed to say "no" to my CEO because I want to be effective? That's a complicated question, obviously, but no matter how we answer that question, we do need some method for prioritizing these requests. And this method should involve a way of maximizing our effectiveness, which is defined by Drucker as answering this question, "What is the most important contribution I can make to the performance of this organization?"

Let's recap.

Not knowing what to work on next causes stress and prevents us from being effective. This is no way to live. I wrote this book because marketers should be able to enjoy the work they do, believe that it makes a difference, and work at a pace that is just the right level of stress and challenge. For good measure, throw in some time to take a run before work and be home in time for dinner with the family. This is not too much to ask.

What is Agile and Why it Matters

What is agile? The term is thrown around too loosely. Those that choose to understand it more eventually discover the *Manifesto for Agile Software Development*. Then, once we get to the term "software development," especially marketers, we stop and say, "Well, this isn't for me. I'm not a software developer." If you read the manifesto, you realize that it is highly accessible to anyone, no matter what type of work they do. Including marketers. In fact, a small group of marketers got together and wrote the *Agile Marketing Manifesto*.

I will not spend too much time on the manifestos because they have been written about in plenty of other places, which I cite later in this chapter. But, I will say this. These manifestos are philosophies that describe, plainly, a set of beliefs that guide the way work should be done. Agile, by itself, is not a method of working.

Agile is a belief system.

Within the agile belief system, there are several methodologies that one can use to apply the agile belief system. These methodologies include:

- Scrum
- Kanban

- Scrumban (oh, good grief)
- Extreme programming
- Adaptive software development
- Feature-driven development
- Pragmatic programming
- Lean development

This is a partial list to give you an idea of the choices we have in how we choose to apply agile. In this book, I focus on two methodologies. Kanban and scrum. Actually, I focus on scrum, but since my agile journey began with kanban, I spend plenty of time describing kanban and how I use it in Jira.

For now, here is the key take away. Agile is a belief system. Kanban and Scrum are agile methodologies.

Got it? Sort of? Almost? I understand. You will get it, and you will clearly understand how to apply it to your work by the time you finish reading this book.

Benefits of Agile

Now that you know what agile is, let's talk about the benefits of agile. James S. Wright has a list of excellent and relatable benefits in his book *Scrum Marketing: Applying Agile Methodologies to Marketing*.

When you start working in an agile way, specifically using Scrum, you gain the following benefits, says Wright:

Increased flexibility to meet changing market conditions
Improved priority setting
Creating an environment for getting more work done in the same amount of time
Empowering people to say "yes" to the important things and "no" to the less important things

Shifting decisions from "the way we do things" to "what's best for our customers" based on validating learning
Amplified value to planning, accountability, transparency, and increased communication

How does this list apply to you? For me personally, Wright had me at empowering people to say "no" to the less important things. I love saying "no" to things, even though I am not very good at it.

Agile marketing will not magically make all of your problems go away. Hardly. The point here is that anyone can do agile to improve effectiveness at work. Agile is not technical. Agile is not reserved for the rarified air of software developers. In his book, *Scrum: The Art of Doing Twice the Work in Half the Time,* Jeff Sutherland, co-creator of scrum, tells stories about how people have used scrum to plan weddings and kitchen remodels. Parents have used scrum to help their kids do school work. Seriously. Kids. School. Work. Does that sound technical to you?

Scrum is actually quite simple, as you will learn. It's just not so easy to stick to.

James Wright compares agile to adopting an exercise and fitness program. "It is not expensive or difficult to do. It is challenging to keep the commitment to changing your habits, sticking to the new programs, and becoming a fit person."

Scrum is not expensive or difficult to do. You can do scrum with sticky notes, a Sharpie, and a nice open wall in your office (or in your living room). It is better with Jira, especially if you have a team, but you can do it with sticky notes. In fact, I recommend later in the book that you should run your first scrum project with sticky notes and a wall in the office to get some experience doing it with as little effort as possible.

Agile methods (scrum and kanban, as two examples) are needed because, as James Wright describes in his list of benefits, they provide a means for marketing teams to prioritize work, deliver work more quickly and predictably, and provide a process for when to say "yes" and when to say "no" to work.

Why I wrote this book

I wrote this book for two reasons. First, I have a burning desire to help people learn new skills and do their jobs better. This desire comes from my background in employee learning and development, during which I helped literally thousands of people learn new technology skills and earn industry licenses and credentials that are both resume building and career changing. Imagine the satisfaction and sense of accomplishment someone gains when they learn a new software tool or pass an industry licensing examination, especially when they didn't think they could. These are the moments in life that change people. They enable people to get a new job, a raise, a promotion so they can improve their standard of living and sense of self-worth. "I did that, and now I can do this."

I am not trying to change the world. I just like helping one person learn one thing and do one thing. This is the higher purpose of my work in helping people use software to do their jobs.

This book is my attempt to help marketing professionals learn a new way of working (agile) and learn to use technology that is new to them (Jira, Confluence, Jira Service Desk).

Put that on your resume and vape it.

The second reason I wrote this book is to help people understand "how" to implement the agile methodologies scrum and kanban in Jira Software, Confluence, and Jira Service Desk. The book is designed to provide sufficient detail that someone could, after reading this book, start a scrum project the next day. That is how specifically useful I designed this book to be.

It is not that I am an expert in agile marketing. There are plenty of true experts out there. In fact, there is no shortage of information about agile, agile marketing, and the specific agile methodologies. There is the *Agile Manifesto for Software Development* and the *Agile Marketing Manifesto*. There are many excellent books about agile, agile marketing, and scrum. *The Death of Marketing* by Andrea Fryrear, *Hacking Marketing* by Scott Brinker, and the definitive guide to scrum, *Scrum: Doing Twice the Work in Half the Time* by the co-creator of scrum, Jeff Sutherland, and James S. Wright's book, *Scrum Marketing: Applying Agile Methodologies to Marketing.*

These are excellent books. You should read them. I have read them, and I reference them throughout this book. There is only one problem with these books. They do not cover how to implement agile methodologies. They cover why agile is important and why you should do it. They also cover what to do. They just don't cover how.

I wrote this book to cover "how." I am making the assumption in this book that you already know why you should do agile marketing and even what you need to do. You just don't know how to do it.

This book will show you how, specifically how to implement kanban and scrum using the Atlassian suite of software products, Jira Software, Confluence, and Jira Service Desk.

I believe, after you read this book, you will feel confident that you could implement scrum on your team and do it in Jira. At the very least, you will say to yourself, "I think I could actually do this, and I think it will actually work."

How you will understand how

This book does not tell you how to do it. This book is more about how our team at ServiceRocket does it. I will tell our story warts and all. I will not sugarcoat how we do it or our results. We don't do agile perfectly. We have made many mistakes, and we have plans for improving how we use it.

I will share all of those. I believe that by sharing how we did it, you will learn that you don't have to do it perfectly either. You can start small, gain some momentum, and build upon your success.

The sooner you begin and the more you practice the elements of scrum (daily scrum, sprint planning, sprint review, retrospective, backlog grooming, estimating) the faster you will learn. And the more you learn the better you will get at scrum.

There are many ways to implement agile marketing, and you know your team and culture better than I do and what would work in your organization better than I do. So, I will not presume to tell you what to do. I will, however, tell you our story. Take from it what you like and ignore what you don't.

Create your own art.

I hope this book motivates you to try something new. To try a process that can help you climb out of the pit of the constant barrage of things you could work on, take command of your work, set your own agenda, and maximize your contribution to your organizations and minimize the stress you endure while doing it.

What is in this book

I write about the pesky little details that no one wants to talk about in public. The trade-offs and pain caused by decisions we made that we thought, at the time, were genius. The things most Atlassian expert consultants will warn you about, but you don't listen. I hope to help you learn from our mistakes so you make fewer of them.

This is a book about a marketing team that uses scrum to get work done. I am not going to tell you stories about how smart we are or hipster or cool because we use scrum. Or about how much kale, coconut water, and Philz Coffee we consume. Or how glamorous our lives are because we use scrum.

No.

This is about how frazzled we are...how we struggle with focusing on the most important work and ignoring the urgent unimportant. And how we started using scrum as a means of being able to say to ourselves. "I feel like I know what I'm doing in my work and that I believe I mostly maximize my contribution to the company and to our customers and to each other as a team."

Scrum, the agile methodology

This book is also about scrum, the agile methodology. Although I will spend time describing what scrum is, I will keep that part brief. I will assume most of you know what scrum is, but just cover the basics in the context of how we use it in our work. And to keep continuity in the book for people who don't know what scrum is. If you want to dive deeper into scrum, read the book, *Scrum: The Art of Doing Twice the Work in Half the Time*, and also read the free PDF, *The Scrum Guide: The Definitive Guide to Scrum: The Future of the Game*.

Scrum is one of those things that is quite simple to understand, but difficult to implement well.

I will expose those difficulties in the chapter on how we use scrum.

How we work, day-to-day, in the real world, warts and all

This book is about how we use scrum in our day to day work. I will tell stories about what our meetings look like, how scrum works for us and how we fail to use it properly. I'll also share the mistakes we made along the way. This is not a book of perfection. This is a book of reality.

How a marketing team uses Atlassian tools

This is also a book about how we use the Atlassian suite to run scrum. We use Jira Software, Confluence, and Jira Service Desk to plan, create, track, and deliver almost all of our work. And how we do so in a transparent way. We work out loud and anyone in the company, who wants to, can see what we are working on by following our Confluence space.

How this book is organized

Part 1
In part one, I cover how I got started in agile marketing by implementing kanban in Jira to run the blog at ServiceRocket. I walk through the thought process, implementation, Jira configuration, mistakes, lessons learned and how this process led our team to start using scrum. There are many differences between kanban and scrum, and part one of this book will help you decide which one is right for you.

Part 2
Part two is where we get technical. Not that kind of technical, but the kind of technical that is the practical how of kanban and scrum in Jira and Confluence. Chapter four defines scrum. If you already know what scrum is, skip this chapter. If you do not, read it. It is a primer on scrum written in language marketers will understand. Chapter five describes the Atlassian software tools used for kanban and scrum. These tools include Jira Software, Confluence, and Jira Service Desk.

In chapters six through eight, I describe how we set up each of the three software tools, Jira Software, Confluence, and Jira Service Desk. I show examples of how we configure each. I do not show screenshots and specific features. Those go out of date too fast. I describe our settings conceptually and in a functional way, so that when you get Jira, you will know what to do and how to do it.

In the final chapter of part two, chapter nine, I tell a story about how our team really works in scrum and in the Atlassian software. I share the things we do and don't do and why. This is a valuable chapter because you will learn that it's ok not to do certain things. You may also learn that you should do something that we don't. I would love that.

Part 3

In part three, we round out our agile marketing journey. In chapter ten I describe the mistakes we made, and we made a lot of mistakes. I hope you learn to avoid our mistakes. I also hope you learn that it's ok to make mistakes. In chapter 11, I describe the changes we plan to make in how we do agile marketing. We are still learning and continue to evolve and change how we apply agile principles to our work. Chapter 11 reflects those plans. In chapter 12, I provide for you an example implementation plan. This is the one place where I tell you how to implement agile marketing. Actually, I provide a plan. Take it or leave it. Use it or not. Alter it for your needs. Use it to make your implementation better. In chapter 13, I send you off with a motivational pitch for implementing agile, with a focus on starting small, starting now, and not striving for perfection.

The outcomes you will achieve after reading this book

I intend for this book to help you achieve three broad outcomes. First, is to decide which agile methodology to start with. Second, is to set up Jira Software and Confluence. Third, is to start implementing agile on your team.

After reading this book, you will be able to:

- Select a specific agile methodology to run on your marketing team: kanban, scrum or both
- Set up kanban on Jira Software
- Set up scrum on Jira Software
- Set up a space in Confluence on which you will create all of your work
- Set up Jira Service Desk
- Do agile, so you can become agile

1. Start Small. But Start

"The ability to learn faster than your competitors is the only sustainable competitive advantage."

~ Arie de Geus

This is the story of why, what, and how I started using kanban in Jira to manage the ServiceRocket blog. First of all, the most important lesson in this chapter is this: I started small.

Even before I was in marketing, I was in marketing. I joined ServiceRocket in 2013 to manage the training services line of business, helping software companies build and run their customer education businesses. That was my day job. On the side, I was the primary blog writer for the ServiceRocket blogs.

I got into marketing by writing blogs. My background is in learning and development, helping people learn the skills of their job and the tools needed to do their job. I have done that mostly at technology companies throughout my career. That background is only useful in so far as it sets up my transition to marketing and why I started writing blog posts and ebooks for ServiceRocket.

Leveraging my background in learning, I wrote mostly useful and educational blogs about how software companies can improve customer education. As I wrote blogs and ebooks, I needed a better way to track progress, collect ideas, see what work is ready to be published, and whether there was anything in the pipeline. I needed a better way to visualize how far along I was, especially as I had multiple blogs and even more than one ebook in progress at the same time.

I also needed a way to see what the next steps were so I knew what to work on next. For example, If I knew I had already written the outline, done the research, and taken notes on the research for each item in the outline, I needed a way to know that the next step was to write the rough draft. I knew in my head this was the next step, but because I was so busy, I wanted a process that I could follow so my blog writing was more predictable.

I created a simple process for writing a blog post that looked like this:

- Step 1: Decide on a topic
- Step 2: Write the outline
- Step 3: Do research/Take notes from research
- Step 4: Write first draft
- Step 5: Write complete draft
- Step 6: Final draft

Every time I would write a blog post, I created a task for each of these steps in Jira, and I would generally do one task every day of the week and each week I would write one blog. Sometimes, I had a brilliant idea for a blog post before I finished a current post and added tasks for that one. Over time, I may have five or six blogs in progress and ideas for several more. And I created a task in Jira for all of those.

You can imagine that things were getting overwhelming. Now, every time I logged in to Jira, I would see a long list of tasks and sit there, looking at my screen saying to myself, "What do I work on now?"

I tried a few things to prioritize my work. I sorted the list of blogs by due date. I tried to prioritize the list by which blog was closest to being done. Or I randomly skipped from blog to blog writing here and there in each blog when and where I had inspiration. All of these attempts to prioritize my work failed because I was all over the place.

I needed a way to visualize my list of things to do, so that I could:

- Have a place to put my ideas
- Visualize the work in progress
- Know when I had too many things in progress or not enough in progress

The agile marketing methodology, kanban, addresses these needs very well. Let's talk about how.

Basic concepts in kanban

Kanban is an agile methodology that has three basic elements:

- Visualize workflow
- Limit work in progress
- Pulling work into the workflow

Visualize workflow

Kanban allows you to visualize your work on a board made up of columns that each represents a step in a workflow. Take the example of a simple workflow:

- To Do
- In Progress
- Done

Your kanban board would have three columns. One for each of these steps in your workflow. All of the tasks you have not started yet, show up in your *To Do* column. The tasks you are currently working on show up in the *In Progress* column. Completed tasks are placed in the *Done* column.

Every day, you look at your board and you can see what you finished, what work is in progress right now, and the work you will start on soon. The beauty of a kanban board is that you can look at it and quickly understand where your work stands.

Limit work in progress (WIP)

Kanban is designed to help you concentrate on WIP, minimize multi-tasking, and maximize focus on as few tasks as possible to make sure progress is made and work is getting done. The idea is to limit the amount of work in progress so you do not start too many tasks at once and end up not accomplishing anything.

Pulling work into the workflow

As you complete work in progress and the number of tasks that are in that column dwindles, you easily see that you need to put more work in progress. And visually, you effectively "pull" work from the To Do column to the WIP column because you see that it is empty. It will naturally make you think to yourself, "Uh oh. I need to start on new tasks because the board is showing that we are running out of work in progress."

I recommend starting with kanban because it will help you get used to working in a flow state, working on a board, managing a backlog (the To Do column), pulling work through a workflow, getting through the struggles of having too many things in progress, and not having anything in progress. Starting with kanban is also relatively simple to do with a small team or even for an individual.

When I started with kanban, I was an individual. Over time, I added people to the board who helped with creating writing ideas and doing the writing.

That is kanban at a high level. There are lots of details, but you can get started with kanban knowing just what I describe above. In fact, you can do it with a whiteboard and sticky notes. Grab a pen, draw three columns, label them with your workflow (To Do, In Progress, Done), write down all of your tasks on sticky notes, and stick those on the board in the To Do column. Then, just start moving tasks over as you work on them and complete them.

You could do that. And you should do that for your first project because it will help you get started and gain some experience using the kanban methodology. Since this is a book about how to do agile marketing in Jira, I will show you how I created a kanban board in Jira.

How I set up my kanban board in Jira

Although I was a Jira user when I started using kanban, I was not familiar with the kanban features in Jira. So, I asked Matt Doar to set this up for me. Matt Doar is a staff engineer at Linkedin and the co-author of the book, *Practical Jira Administration: Using Jira Effectively Beyond the Documentation*. When I asked Matt to help me, he was the chief toolsmith at ServiceRocket and our leading Jira technical consultant. As you can image, Matt Doar is an expert.

He willingly helped me, and I think he was genuinely excited about the opportunity to help a business user like me get up and running in an agile methodology in Jira.

Below, I describe how he set up my kanban board. Later in the book, I describe the different features in detail, so that you know what is possible. Here, as I describe how we set up the kanban board in Jira, I will keep it at a high level.

Set up a project

The first thing Matt Doar created for me was a project in Jira. A project is a place in Jira in which work occurs on a specific project, topic, or distinct type of work. We called the project "Communications." I wanted the name to be as simple as "The Blog" but Matt recommend we make it broader in case we wanted to start doing more, other, similar type of work that was not just writing a silly blog. I listen to smart people.

Permissions

The next thing we did was set permissions for the project so that anyone at ServiceRocket could have access. The project was created in our company-wide Jira instance. Everyone at ServiceRocket has access to this Jira. There are many times when we have employees who are not in marketing but are subject matter experts and would either write or review content. We wanted to share any issues in the project with anyone at ServiceRocket and ask them to contribute.

For example, a consultant might want to write a blog post summarizing an interesting challenge they solved for a client. The marketing team would see this and then collaborate on the issue to get it written and published.

We generally have an open culture at ServiceRocket so it was easy to make this decision. But understand that you can up your permissions to be as open or closed as necessary. In general, it is good practice to limit access to the people who should have access and no more, but there is no right way to do this. There is just the way that suits your company and culture. The point is that Jira is flexible and allows you to define whatever permissions you want.

Issue Type

Then we created one custom issue type. An issue type is a task, and on that task, there are fields that need to be filled out to describe what the task is. In the interest of ease and simplicity, we created one issue type called, "Blog." On the Blog issue type we created five fields:

Summary: This is the subject line for the issue type. It is a one-liner that describes the content piece. We used this as the working headline for the piece.

Assignee: Here is where we assigned the issue to the person who would write it.

Description: The description field is a large open field on which you can write anything. Here is where we would write a few paragraphs describing the content of the piece. Things like: Intended audience, goals for the piece, a short description, what the format of the piece would be, any links to resources or research, or anything else to help people understand what the piece is about.

Due date: Estimated date at which the piece is expected to be published.

Label: A label is a keyword. We used these to categorize content pieces by line of business or topic.

Every time we create an issue to write a blog, we fill out these fields to describe what the blog is, who will do it, and when it is due. Then we add a link to the page on Confluence, where we write the blog.

More on Confluence later in the book.

Create a workflow

Next, we created a workflow, which describes the steps in the process a blog goes through to get done. Our workflow has the following five steps:

Ideas: We called the first step "ideas" because we wanted a place to store ideas for the blog. Whenever we have an idea for a blog or a guide or even a webinar, any content piece really, we create an issue. All new issues are listed in the "Ideas" workflow step.

In Progress: Once we start working on an issue, we move it to "In Progress" on the kanban board, you simply drag the issue across the columns to "In Progress."

Ready for Review: Once content is written, it is moved to the "Ready for Review" stage and then it can be assigned to the person who needs to review it.

Approved by Creator: This stage is when the issue is sent back to the writer of the content so they can approve the changes made by the person who edited it. This step was designed to check the checker.

Published: Once a content piece is published, it is moved to this stage, which is the equivalent of closing the issue or otherwise marking it complete.

These are just five stages we came up with. The beauty of Jira is that we can create these five workflow steps and name them whatever we want. For example, instead of calling the final step "Done," I called it "Published."

Set up the kanban board

What I described above are some of the basic Jira functionality we used to set up our project. After all of that is done, we need to set up the kanban board so we can start visualizing the work on the project. A kanban board is a way to visualize the flow of work from "Idea" to "Published." So, by looking at our board every day, I can tell what tasks are in progress, in review, or published.

I can also tell when there is nothing in progress. This might be one of the most useful elements of using a kanban board. You can actually "see" when work is not flowing. For example, if you are working on a lengthy ebook or white paper, it is very easy to get so focused on writing, editing, and designing the book, that when you finally get done, you realize, the next "thing" has not been started because there are no tasks in the "In Progress" column. Simply by looking at your Jira kanban board, you can easily see that nothing is in progress. It makes it easy for you and your team to say, "Hey, we have nothing in progress for the next project, we should make a decision on what to start on next."

This is how we created our kanban board.

Columns

One foundational principle in kanban is the columns. This is where the visual layout comes into play. The best way to set up your columns is to have your columns match your workflow steps.

Remember from the example above, our workflow steps are:

- Ideas
- In Progress
- In Review
- Approved by Creator
- Published

To configure the board, we will create a column for each of these workflow steps. In fact, when you start creating columns, Jira will ask you to match a workflow step with a column. That way, when you move an issue from "Ideas" to "In Progress," the issue will be moved on the kanban board from the "Ideas" column to the "In Progress" column. Naturally, you want your columns to match your workflow steps.

You can change the name of your column headers. For example, consider the name of our first workflow step, "Ideas." You could change the name of the column for all of your ideas and call it "Things to do." For the "In progress" column, you could name the column "Working on it."

The point is that you can. You don't have to.

Honestly, I don't know why you'd want to do this, but we are people and we are crazy and we like to make things more complicated than they need to be. Maybe you want to do this just for fun. Maybe just because you can. Maybe you can think of a good reason. I cannot.

Swimlanes

Swimlanes are rows on your kanban board that allow you to categorize the issues on your board. This adds an additional visual element to your kanban board. With columns, you can easily see the flow of issues through your board. With swimlanes, you can visualize the issues by certain categories of work. Here's what I mean:

Each swimlane (row) represents a category of some kind. The categories could be:

By Assignee (who owns the issues): Show all of Kim's issues in this swimlane and Joe's issues in the next swimlane. You could have a swimlane for each person on the team.

By Issue Type: Show a certain type of work in this swimlane. Show all blog posts in this swimlane and white papers in that swimlane.

By Team: Put all of Field/Event Marketing in one swimlane. Content marketing in that swimlane. A swimlane for each team.

By Project: Show all tasks for that white paper project in this swimlane. All projects for an event in another swimlane.

Swimlanes are an important concept because as the number of issues grows, and you have scores or even hundreds of open issues, it can be very difficult to sort through it all. Setting up swimlanes helps you sort through it all.

This is where the art comes into play. We configured our swimlanes by due date. As the list of issues grew, it was challenging to know what issues to work on next. To help us know what to work on next, we wanted to automate what work to pull into the in-progress stage. We chose to do it by due date.

We created two swimlanes.

1. Due This week
2. Everything Else

Due this week: The swimlane on top of our kanban board is called "Due This Week" and shows only the issues that are due this week. This focuses our attention on these issues for obvious reasons. One of the cool things about this swimlane is that it will show the issues that are due this week but have not been started. It creates some urgency and we can mobilize and get the work done. Without this view, it is easy to forget some tasks that just show up on the long list of blog ideas.

How many times have you come into the office and realized, "Oh my gosh, the newsletter needs to go out today!" This type of swimlane helps us minimize surprises like this.

Everything else: Simply put, any tasks not due this week, are just placed in the second swimlane. This swimlane is basically our list of issues that we will someday get to.

As you can tell, there are many ways to set up swimlanes. We kept it simple. You can, too. But you don't have to. You can create swimlanes by categories and sort your issues by a wide variety of work types to suit your needs.

Card layout

Each task on the kanban board is represented by a rectangular card, like a sticky note on a whiteboard. In these cards are listed the name of the issue and who it is assigned to. This is the default setting. You can change this. Maybe you want to add due date to the card so you can see the due date. Maybe you want to add the name of the person who created the issue. The point is that you can decide what you want to put on that card to make viewing it on the board more useful to you. We kept the default settings, name, and assignee.

Card colors

Each card can also be assigned a color based on criteria in Jira. For example, all blog issue types are green, all event issue types are blue, and all sales enablement issue types are purple.

That is just one example.

We do it by due date. And we have three criteria.
1. All issues due in more than a week (or have no due date assigned to them yet) are green.
2. All issues due in the next week are orange.
3. All issues due in one week or less, or are overdue are, you guessed it, red.

Working days

You can set working days for your board. If you use any of the date related criteria, like we do, setting working days is important.

For example, if you want to show issues in a swimlane that are due in the next 5 days, and you have a holiday coming up, you can set certain days so that they do not count towards that. We set working days to Monday through Friday and then added our company holidays as non-working days.

Issue detail view

The inside detail view is the equivalent of a preview. Instead of opening up an issue in full, you can click on a card and see a preview of the issue. You do this to get a quick detail view of the task without having to open up the entire issue screen.

The point here is that you can define what fields you want to show on that detail view. You can choose to display all fields on that view, which may overwhelm the preview or you can show a minimal view. The point is you have a choice. We keep it fairly minimal and show the following fields on our issue detail view:

- Status
- Labels
- Due Date
- Created
- Updated
- Reporter
- Assignee
- Linked Issues

Those are the basic settings we used to set up our kanban board.

How we set up kanban and how you should

I do not claim this is how kanban should be set up in Jira, only that this is how we did it. I have a bias towards simplicity and minimalism. So, my customizations were few. My setup may not work for you. I believe, the best way to help you learn how to set up your kanban board in Jira is to show how I did it. Honestly, I hope you read my description above and said, "Oh, that would never work for me because I need to be able to see the tasks in this way." That is perfect. Jira can, almost certainly, be set up to help you "see the tasks in this way."

On the other hand, you would do yourself a huge favor if you set up Jira exactly how I describe above, and just started working. No thinking. Just action. That way, you will gain experience in both Jira and kanban, while at the same time discovering particular needs you and your team have. Then you can make adjustments to your configuration as you learn how kanban can work for you.

Don't think about setting up your kanban board in Jira as a "set it and forget it" task. You should adjust your configuration as your team changes and grows, and as you learn. It is way more important to get started than it is to get your setup just right.

On Jira configurability

The thing about Jira is that it is highly configurable. You can set it up in almost any way possible, which is both a good and a bad thing. If you buy Jira and don't customize anything you can work just fine, but the default settings might not make sense to you because of the language used in the default settings. If you over-customize it to be precisely how your team is structured and works today, when things change (and you know they will change) your configuration may actually become friction in your team's work and will actually make your team less flexible. You will want to find a balance and be biased towards less customized. I will spend more time on the customization topic later in the book.

2. Kanban Was Great, but...

"Open your eyes. Look within. Are you satisfied with the life you are living?"

~ Bob Marley

As our marketing team grew, our work changed. Our marketing became multi-dimensional. We were branching out beyond content marketing, which was an early strength, into improving our marketing automation, email marketing, paid media, event marketing, and community engagement. Planning, tracking, and doing all this work on a kanban board started to overwhelm us because our backlog of work showing on the kanban board in the ideas column was way too long to be practical.

At the time, Mark Gopez, then head of marketing for Gliffy, a software company that allows you to draw diagrams and flowcharts very easily, told me his marketing team used another agile methodology called scrum. I was intrigued to learn more because I learned about scrum on my agile learning journey but initially thought it was for software teams. But when Mark told me his marketing team used scrum, I wanted to learn more.

I took a trip to the Gliffy office in San Francisco with my colleague, Colleen Blake, then VP of marketing at ServiceRocket, and we sat through Mark's retrospective meeting. As you will learn later in this book, a retrospective meeting is a meeting during which the team reviews how their last phase of work went. The entire meeting addresses three questions:

1. What worked?
2. What did not work?
3. What can we do better next time?

There are variations to these three question, but basically that's it. That's the meeting.

The first thing I noticed in the meeting was that they were so calm and organized. In one exchange, they were discussing tasks that did not get completed.

"Why not?" Mark asked.

"I underestimated how long it would take to complete this task. It took me a lot longer than I thought. And then when that new project came in that we had to do that we had not planned for, there was no way I was going to get this one done."

Estimated? I thought. Who estimates their work? And why does that matter? New tasks we hadn't planned for? Aren't there always new tasks that we don't plan for? The team seemed so calm and organized, especially while discussing work that didn't get done. They seemed to know why the work did not get done. The discussion was not so much about why the task did not get done, but how could they either have anticipated the extra work and/or estimated better. In other words, the discussion was not about why the content marketing manager did not get her work done, it was about why the work did not get done in the context of the process and the environment and the unexpected.

The content marketing manager went on. "Even though that new tasks came in, I still think we underestimated the work in this sprint in the first place. I think this other task should have been eight story points, not five. I can normally do 25 points in a sprint but this time, I only completed 20."

OK. That's good to know, I thought. What's a story point? I was amazed and baffled and inspired because they spent this meeting talking about how to improve how they work so they can be a little better next time. Who does this? Scrum teams. That's who.

As I left that meeting, I thought a lot about how we use kanban. For us, kanban really improved our blog quality and production. Kanban gave us a place to collect ideas. We always knew what was in progress. We knew when we had too many tasks in progress, which was slowing us down. Finally, we also could easily tell when we didn't have anything in the pipeline and could better predict when we might miss a publishing deadline.

Moreover, the way we set up our kanban board in Jira Software, we could take contributors from all over the company to write. Plus, we could pull in reviewers and subject matter experts to contribute to checking and improving the blogs. This was so successful that we wondered whether we could apply this process to all of our marketing work. Event planning, creative, go to market planning, customer stories. and other work.

After sitting through the meeting with Mark's team, I realized scrum would be a better method for running our marketing work. For a few reasons.

First, they seemed so calm and organized and on top of it about work not getting done. They also seemed to have a method for dealing with new urgent tasks thrown at the team at the last minute and how that impacted the work they had already planned. They seemed to focus more on the issue of unplanned work versus planned work and how to "plan" or estimate it better next time, than in discussing why something didn't get done or even looking for blame. They seemed very focused on the process and improving the process.

Second, they had a method for planning work. They called it estimating. They had estimated their work and then reviewed how they estimated it. In the story above, they didn't estimate as well as they should have. They acknowledged that, and then they talked about how to estimate better the next time. I found that liberating.

At the time, it was odd to me that their estimates did not include hours. They did not seem to track hours. Which is a relief because I really don't want to log time like I did when I was a consultant. On the other hand, I thought, how else does one estimate work except by hours and due date deadlines? We will soon find out.

Third, the team gave themselves self-imposed deadlines. The deadline for all the work they planned had ended that day. What I did not notice at the time was that they planned all of their work two weeks before in a planning meeting. The team sat down with each other, planned all the work they would do in the next two weeks, and basically promised each other they could get all that work done in the next two weeks. The retrospective meeting seemed to mark the end of that two-week period.

If you had to go into a meeting next Thursday and talk about all the work you got done in the previous two weeks and explain why you did not do some work, you'd probably get the work done. Or at least have a good explanation why you did not get it done. That's basically what the Gliffy marketing team did every two weeks. It all seems so calm and organized, and I wanted some of that.

That visit inspired our marketing team to try scrum. We did not start scrum the next day, but we did start socializing it with the team that we might soon try this new work process called scrum.

Why scrum?

There are many reasons to use scrum, but let's start with two practical reasons that I learned from our visit to Gliffy.

1. Time bound work cycles.
2. A process to help us focus on the most important work.

Let's talk about each.

Reason #1: Time bound work cycles

One of the important concepts in scrum, in my opinion, is the sprint. A sprint is a pre-defined period of time during which a concrete and specific amount of work is planned and completed. The analogy is the aid station in an ultramarathon. When you run an ultramarathon, it can be overwhelming to think about running 30 or 50 or 100 miles. One effective strategy to overcome that barrier is to break down the race into smaller distances and focus attention on the next short distance. Ultramarathons (like most other running races) have aid stations. In an ultramarathon, aid stations may be spaced out anywhere from three to fifteen miles apart. The idea is to say to yourself, "It's just five miles to the next aid station. Just go five miles. Just get to the next aid station."

Sprints in scrum are just like that. If you are planning your biggest event of the year, let's say, your user conference, it is daunting to think you can pull that off. You have to break that up into smaller work chunks for such a thing to even be fathomable. This is where the sprint comes in.

A sprint is usually one to four weeks, depending on your preference, and you only plan work for the current sprint. Work that you know you can deliver and that will get you one step closer to being ready for that event. For example, instead of thinking about booking a keynote speaker, which can be daunting. You plan that in the next two weeks you will:

- Make a list of possible speakers categorized by dream speakers to "safe school" speakers.
- Finalize budget for keynote speaker.
- Call top three speakers to request the booking.

These are very doable tasks within the bigger task of booking a keynote speaker. These are actions that can get done in the next two weeks, and they are important actions that move the needle, advance the overall project AND (perhaps most importantly) provide the team a sense of accomplishment at the end of a sprint cycle.

This is the equivalent to "getting to the next aid station." Wow. I made it.

The sprint cycles and time-bound nature is one of the most important reasons we wanted to start using scrum. Because it provides a sense of urgency, forces us to break down bigger tasks, and allows us to experience a sense of achievement.

Reason #2: A process to help us focus on the most important work

The second reason we chose scrum is that scrum affords a process by which we can prioritize and focus on important things more often than urgent things. At the time of this writing, we are a marketing team of seven people running marketing initiatives for three lines of business, a dozen or so product families, and scores of individual products and services from consulting services to software products. We find it a challenge (understatement of this book) to focus on the most important work.

We figured scrum would help us focus on the most important work. The sprint planning and retrospective process are the keys to doing this. We start each sprint with a meeting to decide what we will all work on during that two-week period known as the sprint. That meeting will help us make conscious decisions about what we would work on, question why we were working on certain things, and make conscious decisions to not work on certain things during a particular sprint.

Once we have planned our next two weeks, we know exactly what to work on and why we are working on it. We also have a higher degree of confidence that we will finish it all because we made deliberate decisions on what and when.

We will also be ready when others in the company come to us and ask, "Why are you running a campaign for this product?" or, "Can you please send an email out tomorrow about this product enhancement?"

This sprint planning process allows us to say, "Sorry. Our sprint is locked down, we will put your request in the backlog and get to it in a future sprint." Of course, this is easier said than done. But at least we have some basis for making that statement and asking the requester to justify to us why their request is important enough to "interrupt" our well-planned sprint.

As Scott Brinker describes in his book, *Hacking Marketing: Agile Practices to Make Marketing Smarter, Faster, and More Innovative,* sprint planning "keeps marketing more plan driven and less interruption driven." The day will come when your product team comes to you and asks if you can run some campaign "this week" on a new product enhancement. Without a well-planned sprint, a typical marketing team would need to either take on the new work or argue against it and risk looking like an unhelpful marketing team.

An agile marketing team running scrum takes a different approach. Brinker suggests saying, "We're in the middle of a sprint right now. Can this wait until our next sprint—which is less than two weeks away? That way, we can address it in our next sprint planning in the context of other priorities?" Trust me when I say that at first, this will impress your product team because they will not be ready for you to be this plan focused and organized. Most product teams will understand and be happy to get their request in your backlog for planning in a near future sprint. For the teams that still want you to jump on their request immediately, Brinker wants you to respond by saying, "If your request is urgent, we can swap out some tasks in our sprint to make room for your tasks, which tasks do you think we should swap out?" This may require talking to stakeholders, which also may deter the urgent-minded requests.

It is perfectly fine to swap tasks in scrum. According to Brinker, the key is to minimize these swaps and to focus on rebalancing work intentionally, not accidentally.

Most work can wait two weeks, right? Just because we don't think our work can wait two weeks, doesn't meet it cannot. Having the conversations above will allow us to focus more time on important, planned work and provide us a tool for saying "no" to urgent, unplanned requests.

Find your reasons for choosing scrum

We chose scrum for these two reasons:

1. Time bound work cycles.
2. A process to help us focus on the most important work.

There are many other reasons to choose scrum. I hope that as you read the rest of this book, you will discover reasons of your own.

There are also reasons not to choose scrum, but that is not what this book is about.

Part Two [Doing Scrum]

3. What is Scrum

"Training slow has always been considered a sign of weakness or laziness. However, if you want to run, bike, or swim faster, a successful and intelligent approach is to slow down!"

~ Phil Maffetone

When I first starting learning about agile and scrum, I was intimidated because it was created by software developers, for software teams. However, the more I learned, the easier I found the concepts. I thought to myself, "These concepts are easy to understand. Any team can do this. I can plan my kitchen remodel using scrum. I can get my kids to finish their larger homework projects using scrum."

Scrum is not difficult to understand. It is not intimidating at all. It is accessible to any team. Even marketing teams. But scrum is not going to implement itself. So, it is important to understand found things that are difficult about scrum.

Changing how you work: we are used to an old way of working. Learning and doing a new way of anything is difficult.

Sticking to it is difficult: being disciplined about it until it becomes a habit.

Convincing others to do it: it's one thing to do it yourself. It is another thing to convince someone else. Harder to convince a team of 7 or 23.

Just plain getting started: we overcomplicate things...make things see too hard so we don't even start. We can start small and simple and build. We don't have to do everything at once. Starting is hard. Let's make it easy to start.

I wrote this book to help you get over these hurdles, to start on scrum, and to get Jira Software and Confluence up and running. To get your team to start, I want to help you make starting easier because I know that once you start, you will keep going and become an expert in scrum. Once you become an expert in scrum, you will lead you team to become more productive and more innovative.

Scrum: The vocabulary

The goal of this book is to show you "how" to implement scrum, not to define what scrum is. Therefore, I don't want to spend much time on what scrum is. However, since the remainder of this book shows you how to implement scrum, I will extensively use scrum vocabulary, and if you have not had any exposure to scrum basics, the rest of the book will be difficult to understand. In this chapter, I explain the major elements of scrum so that when you read the stories later in the book about how we set up scrum in Jira Software, you will know exactly how we did it.

If you know what scrum is, I recommend skipping this chapter and just go to the next one to start learning how we set up Jira Software. You will miss nothing if you skip this chapter.

If you have little or no exposure to scrum, this chapter will give you the basics you need to start using scrum. If, after reading this chapter, you want to go deeper in learning scrum, I recommend reading the following three books:

- *Scrum: The Art of Doing Twice the Work in Half the Time* by Jeff Sutherland. He is the co-creator of scrum and one of the original signers of the Agile Manifesto.
- Also read his *Scrum Guide*. The *Scrum Guide* is free. It's a PDF on the internet. Google that. Find it. Read it.
- *Hacking Marketing: Agile Practices to Make Marketing Smarter, Faster, and More Innovative* by Scott Brinker.
- *The Death of a Marketer: Modern Marketing's Troubled Past and New Approach to Change the Future* by Andrea Fryrear.

You will find that the rules of scrum are quite easy. It's the sticking to the process that's hard, just like forming any new habit.

What is scrum?

Scrum is an agile methodology. It is one application of scrum. It is nothing more than a set of processes that, when followed, add up to a method of working. Let's just start talking about each element of scrum.

Roles

The first element of scrum is that there are roles. This is one difference between kanban and scrum. Kanban does not have specific roles. Scrum does. And the roles are important, just as roles are important on any marketing team, except that in scrum, these are not job titles. These are roles. Any one on your marketing team can assume any one of these roles.

There are three roles on a scrum team:

1. Product owner
2. Team member
3. Scrum master

Let's talk about each.

Product owner: This role owns the outcome of all the work a scrum team produces. On a marketing team this would include content, paid ad copy, sponsorships, events, campaigns, and anything a marketing team produces. The product owner makes final decisions on that output. On our marketing teams, this role could be the CMO, VP, or director of marketing. Or it could be the person who reports to the CMO, VP, or director of marketing. Whoever it is, the product owner needs to have the confidence and authority to make decisions on what your scrum team prioritizes.

Team member: A team member is responsible for developing and delivering all the work the marketing team develops. On the marketing team, this might include product marketing managers, copywriters, graphic designers, and social media marketing specialists. Anyone on a scrum team who is not the product owner or scrum master is a team member.

Scrum master: The scrum master is the equivalent of a project manager who is primarily responsible for ensuring that the scrum process is followed. When the team gets lazy or falls into old habits or ignores some of the scrum processes, the scrum master brings the team back on track. The scrum master is also responsible for clearing the way for the team to deliver on what it planned. When and if there are things in the organization preventing the marketing scrum team from getting the work done, the scrum master clears the way so that the scrum team can deliver. When the scrum master cannot clear the way, the scrum master gets the product owner to go out to the organization to help set priorities.

Roles can be flexible, but...

In an ideal world, each role has at least one dedicated person. In the real world, there could be overlaps. On a small marketing team, each person might take on a few roles. Don't get caught up on having a person for each role. Focus on the responsibilities of each role and executing those responsibilities.

The sprint

Scrum is made up of sprints, which are defined time periods, during which a concrete set of work is delivered. The purpose of a sprint is to plan the work the team can deliver by the end of the sprint. The work should be a clearly defined deliverable that can be shown to a customer or stakeholder as something that is, at a minimum, a prototype or first draft. In a marketing context that could be a draft of a blog post, storyboard of an ad campaign, or a proposal for event sponsorships. Whatever the deliverables, the sprint provides a defined time period during which the work gets done, and then delivered to a customer (internal or external).

Sprints are commonly two-week periods, but you decide the time period that works for you. Sprints can be weekly, monthly, or quarterly. The point is to not make your sprint so short that you cannot complete meaningful work, but not so long that stakeholders wonder what you are doing all day. I think quarterly is way too long. If you can't decide, start with two weeks.

Projects have multiple sprints. For example, a go-to-marketing campaign might take three months to develop. During that time, there may be six, two-week sprints that occur consecutively, at the end of which the product launch is completed.

Sprint planning

Sprint planning happens before (or at the beginning of) each sprint. The team gets together in a meeting to decide what should, and can, get done during the sprint. This is an important process, because each team member is fully in charge of what they commit to in a sprint; not the product owner and not the scrum master. Each team member owns what they commit to. Scrum works so well because team members own their work and how much they commit to for each sprint. A sprint planning meeting is generally a process of reviewing everything that could be done, and then narrowing down what should be done within the sprint.

Once the amount of work is determined, the work for that sprint is locked down. No other work should occur. I know what you are thinking, "Is that even possible?" It is. And it all comes down to the scrum master.

The scrum master is the gatekeeper, keeping all unplanned work out of the sprint. While there will often be escalations and last-minute changes, the scrum master reviews these requests and makes sure there is a darn good reason before allowing the team to work on them. The goal is to keep the sprint focused on *planned* work. The scrum master fights against the unplanned work ensuring it is kept out of the sprint.

The stand up

The stand up (or daily scrum) is a meeting held each day during a sprint, with everyone on the scrum team. The meeting is short. Short enough that standing during the whole meeting doesn't feel too long. Meetings last at most 15 minutes and are ideally held in the same location and at the same time each day. During the meeting, each team member answers the following questions:

What did I accomplish since the last stand up?
What I will accomplish by the next stand up?
What is blocking my progress?

Stand ups keep the team in sync and allow for quick course corrections. These meetings are run by the team, for the team. If a marketing manager comments, "I will finish the copy for the Facebook ad by the next stand up," everyone knows that at the next stand up, she will say whether or not she finished her task. Scrum teams are more collaborative because sprint commitments are to one another on the team, and not to a distant manager or customer.

If the marketing manager shares at the next stand up that her progress is blocked, then it's the role of the scrum master to help remove the blockers. With regular stand ups, everyone knows what's going on, issues are addressed immediately, and the project is more likely to be successful.

The sprint review

The sprint review is a meeting in which the scrum team shows stakeholders what was completed in the sprint. This is the opportunity to show stakeholders what was produced to get feedback from them so the deliverable can be iterated on.

There are many ways to do this meeting. You could schedule individual meetings with stakeholders who need different things from you. You could do an all hands style meeting in which you show your entire company what you completed in the sprint.

Let's look at an example of both.

Let's say your product team is releasing a major new feature, and they want you to promote it to customers and prospects. You agreed to run an integrated campaign which included paid media, email, a webinar, and various other channels. In the first sprint, your team committed to come up with the promotion plan. At the end of that sprint, in your sprint review, you show the promotion plan to the product team. Your plan is your deliverable. You get feedback from the product team. You end the meeting. That's it. For now.

Let's go forward a few sprints. Let's say that in a future sprint, you delivered a Facebook sponsored post inviting people to a webinar. In the sprint review meeting for that sprint, you show the results of the sponsored post. How many clicks, how many webinar signups, how much money was spent, and the conversion rates. You can get feedback from the product team and evaluate how effective the post was.

This isn't the only way to do a sprint review. However you do it, you want to communicate to the right people about what you delivered, collect their feedback, and then take that feedback into your sprint planning meeting and plan future work on iterations, if any.

The retrospective

The retrospective meeting occurs at the end of a sprint. During the retrospective, the team reviews the outcome of the sprint and asks three basic questions:

1. What went well during this sprint?
2. What did not go well during this sprint?
3. What could we improve on for the next sprint?

The retrospective is an opportunity to learn from each sprint, with the purpose of estimating better for the next sprint. When you first start using scrum, you usually find that not everything committed gets accomplished. Why might that happen? We generally overestimate what we can deliver, and under-estimate the urgent tasks and interruptions that occur every day. We find it difficult to say "no," when people ask us do to things, and we end up working on those requests instead of forging ahead on our sprint commitments.

This is normal, and this is why the retrospective is so important. It is a continuous learning process, giving the team a chance to pause and admit, "I did not plan well. I took on too many tasks and was interrupted by the VP of operations who needed an urgent report." The team could respond, "OK, since you create reports for the VP of operations every week, you should plan less work in the sprint. Plan only the work you can do in the sprint." Or the scrum master might say to the VP, "We need to find another way to run your reports because our team needs to focus on this project."

The next sprint should be better because you either commit to less work and actually finish it, or unplanned distractions are removed so you accomplish more in a sprint. This does not always happen perfectly and that's why a retrospective is done frequently, in a process of continuous learning.

The backlog

A backlog is a prioritized list of all the tasks that the marketing team knows they must or might get to sometime in the future. It is your ultimate "to do" list, with all the un-started tasks and ideas related to your project. The scrum difference is that you don't just work through the tasks. Rather, the scrum team pulls work from the backlog, as there is capacity, and assigns the tasks iteratively at the beginning of each sprint.

Backlogs usually go up and down, as work is assigned and completed, and then more tasks are added. Sometimes backlogs grow to be overwhelming because they include potential deliverables, including "someday maybe" items and other wild marketing ideas. Not that marketers ever have those. The scrum master needs to be intimate with the backlog to help determine which tasks belong to which sprint. As your team comes up with new ideas, make sure they don't already exist in the backlog.

You love (or should love) your backlog because it takes the pressure off of having to do everything NOW! Instead, when a new idea comes up, just add it to the backlog. Don't worry about when you should work on that task. That decision is for sprint planning. Each sprint planning meeting is an opportunity to evaluate what's important to work on now, pull those tasks and ideas out of the backlog, and assign them to the current sprint.

We have just learned the big main elements of scrum. As you now understand, the concepts in scrum are not difficult to understand. What's hard is implementing and sticking with the process. Pick a good scrum master. Someone on the team who is process oriented and not afraid to enforce that process.

Do you need to be a scrum master to run scrum?

The scrum master is an important job. It requires that you have someone on your team who owns the process, shepherds your team through scrum and each step in the process. This person should have strong facilitation skills. And the leadership to keep people on it.

As you learn about scrum, you will inevitably come across certified scrum master training programs. Yes, certified scrum master is a thing. It is an industry in itself. So much so, that some people believe strongly that you cannot run scrum without being a certified scrum master.

Don't believe this. You have just read a brief description of the main elements of scrum. I cannot imagine anything you have just learned is so complicated that it requires a certification. You do not need to be a certified scrum master. I'm not, and I run scrum. I started scrum on our marketing team. I had our Jira instance set up to run scrum. I convinced our team to do it. Trust me, there really isn't anything special about my scrum skills. I learned scrum as I went, and as you will read later in this book, I have made plenty of mistakes. I never had scrum training. I read a few books on the topic, all of which I cite throughout this book, and then just started doing it.

Trust me, if you read this book and a few other books about scrum, you will have more than you need to start scrum. You just need to start.

4. The Tools We Use

"The brick walls in the road aren't there to keep you out, they're there to keep everyone else out and give you a chance to prove how much you want it."

~ Randy Pausch

In order to get to the how, we need to understand both the process of scrum, which we've just discussed, and the tools we can use to implement scrum.

In this chapter, I will describe the three main tools our team uses to run scrum. These include Jira, Confluence, and Jira Service Desk. I will summarize each tool and what it does, before I spend the following three chapters describing how we use each tool to implement scrum, so you understand what each tool can do, and how it is designed. This chapter will make the next three chapters easy to understand.

The case for the Atlassian Suite

Before we get into each of the three software tools, and how we use them to run scrum, I want to make the case for why we chose Jira, Confluence, and Jira Service Desk in the first place.

We use these software tools for four main reasons:

1. Flexibility
2. Price
3. Highly configurable
4. Collaborative

Flexibility: The Atlassian Suite of software tools is not just for project tracking. You can use Atlassian products for content management, for providing better service to your stakeholders, for communicating with everyone in your company and with customers. You can add agency partners to your Jira and Confluence projects and spaces and work collaboratively to get work done. Think about that.

Also, you can use the Atlassian products in the cloud, as a service or on-premise. Not every company is buying software in the cloud and Atlassian understands this and provides choice.

Price: Most marketing teams are not very big. Jira doesn't cost that much for small to medium sized teams. Jira starts at a $10 per month flat rate for up to 10 users. Not exactly breaking the bank for a marketing team of four or five people. The same pricing applies to Confluence. Jira Service Desk is a little different because you pay for "agents." An agent is a user who can respond to requests from your customers (internal or external). For $10 per month, you get three agents in Jira Service Desk.

Highly configurable: Where Atlassian software products excel is in configurability. They are designed to adapt to your needs. No matter how complex your team gets, how large, how distributed, Atlassian software will grow with you. You can customize how it looks, how your projects are set up, how work flows through your process, you can even customize the language in Jira to adapt to your team's particular culture, buzzwords, and way of working.

Made for collaboration: Atlassian software is one of the best ways to collaborate with your team and people outside your team in the context of the work you do. When you have a task or a document, you can have all of the conversations about your tasks and documents in Jira and Confluence. You never have to email someone to tell them to review something. You simply mention their name in the task, comments, or document. That person receives a notification and can get on your task or document and respond.

You also never have to email your agency partners and vendors. Ever again. Outside agencies and vendors can be in your Atlassian tools (with the right permissions, of course), performing their work with you. Never send another email to an outside partner again. It really is possible.

This is not a commentary on whether email is good or not. Just that if you use the Atlassian tools, you can have these conversations in the context of the work itself, not in a separate channel, like email. The Atlassian tools allow you to consolidate your work and your communications around that work. This makes you more efficient.

There are many reasons to choose the Atlassian suite. These are the four that mattered to us. To be fair, ServiceRocket is an Atlassian Solutions Partner, so everyone at ServiceRocket uses the tools. In that sense, it was easy to adopt. However, there is nothing preventing us from using other tools, like Trello and Google Docs, which we discussed. But the four reasons I describe above are important to us as a team and made the decision easy.

Now that you understand the reasons we chose Jira, Confluence, and Jira Service Desk, I will go into more detail about what each product can do.

Let's start with Jira.

Jira

Jira is a software product used for tracking tasks and projects. Atlassian created Jira to help software teams keep track of software projects. For many years, Jira was known as a software bug tracker; THE bug tracker. Just as agile was designed by software developers for software development teams, Jira was designed by software developers for software development teams. It was natural that Atlassian built features into Jira so that software teams could implement agile methodologies, like kanban and scrum.

Despite being designed specifically for software teams, Jira has evolved into a task and project tracking product used by teams across many disciplines, including IT help desks, legal, HR, and even marketing teams. Don't be intimidated by Jira's history targeting software teams. Jira has become a product accessible to a wide variety of teams looking to track work in a more collaborative way.

Jira comes in three flavors. Jira Core, Jira Software, and Jira Service Desk. It is important to understand the difference between these three versions of Jira because I recommend you use Jira Software for agile marketing, even though Jira Core is targeted at business teams and Jira Software is targeted at software. I'll explain why.

Jira Core

Jira Core is designed to be a business management project tracking tool to help teams of all kinds run, track, and deliver better projects. Jira Core is targeted at teams like operations, HR, legal and finance and marketing. Although Atlassian is targeting Jira Core to marketing teams, I recommend in this book and show examples from Jira Software, which is targeted at software development teams. The difference between Jira Core and Jira Software is mainly that Jira Software allows you to set up and run agile methodologies like kanban and scrum.

Jira Software

I don't want to give you a marketing lesson or anything. You could probably give me a lesson or two (or three) on marketing. But Atlassian is targeting Jira Software to software development teams that run agile methodologies. After all, software professionals use agile and are the main users of agile methodologies.

As Geoffrey Moore describes in *Crossing the Chasm: Marketing and Selling Disruptive Products to Mainstream Customers*, for Atlassian, the software development team is the beachhead target market on the other side of the chasm. This beachhead target market is also known as the early adopters. Atlassian has done an exceptional job landing that beachhead. Jira has "crossed the chasm" because it is well-adopted among software adoption teams and now other teams in organizations are starting to see the benefits of Jira Software. Marketing teams are looking at Jira Software and agile marketing and starting to think, "We should work like that."

A new generation of marketing professionals is discovering agile and Jira Software to run kanban and scrum. You don't have to be a software development team to use Jira Software. I work on a marketing team and our team uses Jira Software to track everything we do. Jira Software allows us to set up kanban and scrum to run all of our projects. It is really as simple as that. The examples that follow in this book are all done in Jira Software.

Jira Service Desk

Jira Service Desk is the third flavor of Jira, designed to help you set up a "Service Desk." You can take requests from customers and stakeholders and fulfill and track those requests. Think of it this way... You would use Jira Service Desk when someone wants to request business cards, report a problem on the website, or anything else people outside of the marketing team need from marketing. Jira Service Desk allows you to get rid of your marketing@yourcompany.com inbox, which I bet is what you use to handle these types of requests.

Our team uses Jira Software to run our marketing projects, and we use Jira Service Desk to provide service to employees of ServiceRocket who need support from marketing. Said another way, we use Jira Software for our planned work and Jira Service Desk for unplanned work.

Now that you know the difference between Jira Core, Jira Software, and Jira Service Desk, it's time to learn how to set them up. To do that, I will not talk specifically about features. I do not have screenshots in this book. Features and screenshots come and go. I will teach you how to use Jira Software, Confluence, and Jira Service Desk with concepts and real-life examples of how we actually use it. When you understand concepts, figuring out the software is easy. When software is difficult to understand, it is because we don't understand concepts.

Let's now talk about concepts.

Major concepts in Jira Software

To understand Jira Software is to understand each of these major concepts:

- Project types
- Projects
- Issue types
- Permissions
- Notifications
- Workflows

Project types: A project type is a way to categorize all of your projects. Over time, the number of projects in Jira can grow and it is useful, when you view the list of all projects or when you are searching for a certain project, it is easier to find when it is in a category. For a marketing team, you may have several project types like social media, website, content marketing, advertising, events, and product marketing.

Projects: A project in Jira represents a space within which a certain type of work is performed by a certain team of people. It is a discrete location in Jira where this work is sectioned off from other work.

Issue types: An issue is a task. Jira uses the term issue instead of task. Whenever you have some work to do, you create an issue and put it in a project. Think of an issue type as the type of work that you do. In Jira, you can create different types of issues to reflect your work or you can keep it simple. Simple is just having one issue type called task. After all, our day is just a list of tasks we need to get done. A task is a task, right? It has a description, a due date, and who's going to do it. What else is there?

On the other hand, marketing teams have different types of work, right? Content marketing is a type of work. Event marketing is a type of work. Content marketing involves things like editorial calendars and editing and publishing and hiring writers, among many other things. Event marketing involves things like booking space, selecting food and beverage service, name tags, brochures, and sign in sheets. Maybe we want to create custom issue types to reflect the different types of work we do.

For content marketing, you could have several issue types that reflect the actual work you do.

For example:

- Issue Type: Blog
- Issue Type: White paper
- Issue Type: Social media copy
- Issue Type: Webinar
- Issue Type: Workshops
- Issue Type: Ad copy
- Issue Type: Web site copy
- Issue Type: In product copy

Even though a task is a task, we know that writing a blog has different requirements and "sub-tasks" than running a webinar. Jira lets you create a different issue type for a blog than for a webinar to capture those different requirements.

To further this example, event marketing has different types of work which may look something like this:

- Issue Type: Webinar
- Issue Type: Meetups
- Issue Type: Conference sponsorships
- Issue Type: Food and beverage
- Issue Type: Signage, name tags, sign in
- Issue Type: Promotion
- Issue Type: Reminder and follow-up communication
- Issue Type: Presentation content

Why issue types matter

This does look complicated. It is. I am using a complicated example to explain the point you can configure Jira to do a lot of things. The reason you want to create custom issue types is to reflect the type of work your team does and to help your team be more effective. Take the webinar issue type as an example. Planning and running a webinar takes a lot work and has many requirements. When you start to plan a new webinar, you create a new issue in Jira. On that issue, you might need to fill out the requirements like webinar topic, guest speaker, slide content, promotion plan, write webinar description and email reminders, follow up with the recording, etc. With a generic issue type called "tasks" you may not document everything you need to do to run the webinar and forget things. With a custom issue type, you can design the issue so it captures everything you need to plan and run a successful webinar. That's why issue types matter.

Permissions: There are three basic levels of permissions in Jira. One level of permissions decides whether to allow access to your Jira instance. You could set up Jira so that only people on your marketing team have access to it. Or you could set it up so that other people in your organization have access. You could even provide access to vendors, agencies, and contractors to Jira.

A second level of permissions is allowing certain people to have access to certain projects in Jira. You could allow everyone on your marketing team to have access to all projects. Or you can limit which team members have access to what projects. Maybe the content marketing team does not need access to the event marketing project. Larger marketing teams that have a management team could have a project that only the director-level team members have access to. This could be a place where the management team works on more private types of work. You could also create a project specifically for one of your agencies, invite your agency partners into that Jira so that your agencies only see the work in that project.

A third level of permissions is at the issue level. You may want to allow anyone to make any changes to any issue. You may not want someone on the team to change the due date. Maybe you only want the creator of the issue to change the due date (this is just one example). Maybe you don't want anyone to delete an issue. Maybe you don't care. The point is that you can set specific permissions down to the detailed level of creating, changing, and deleting individual issues.

Permissions in Jira is very flexible. With few exceptions, you can address any question related to, "Who can see what and what can they do?"

Notifications: You can set notifications to show up either in Jira and/or send emails when changes are made in Jira. You can turn notifications off, you can send notifications for every change, or set notifications for specific actions. If someone makes a comment on the issue, everyone on that issue can be notified. When someone changes the due date, people can be notified.

Workflows: A workflow is a set of steps that an issue goes through from creation to completion. A simplified workflow looks like this:

To Do > In Progress > Done

You can customize workflows in Jira and even have different workflows for different issue types.

For the blog issue type that we described earlier, we could create a workflow that looks like this:

Idea > First Draft > In Review > Final Draft > Approval > Published

You can have as many or as few steps in the workflow as you want and you can name each step anything you like. Each project can also have their own set of workflows, so each team can create workflows that work for them.

Jira Software is a customizable tool for tracking our work. It is an ideal choice for growing teams looking to implement agile marketing because it is flexible and configurable enough to grow with your team. The only problem with Jira Software is that we don't use it to produce the work. This is what Confluence is for. If Jira Software is for planning and tracking our work, Confluence is for creating that work.

Confluence

Confluence is web-based content collaboration software. You can use Confluence to collaborate around the content and documents and processes for a project. You can use Confluence as a knowledge base, for both employees and customers. You can use Confluence for your company intranet. Confluence has many applications.

Confluence is flexible in that you can make everything open and editable or you can make things read only and even make certain areas in Confluence private and discoverable only to certain people or groups. The beauty of Confluence is in its ability to adapt to your particular needs.

You can use Confluence to create everything you do in marketing. If you need to create a go-to-market plan for a new product, you would create that entire plan in Confluence. You will write all of your blog posts in Confluence. Get them edited and approved. Then publish them on your website. You will publish all of your core marketing processes on Confluence so your team always knows how to do something. You will also create and publish your style guide on Confluence. Basically, 90% of the work you produce will go on Confluence. Why 90%? After you create that booth image for your biggest conference sponsorship of the year, you will still need to create the final image in Adobe Illustrator or similar product. But the concept and copy would be drafted on Confluence.

Confluence is also well-integrated with Jira. When you plan work in Jira, you will link each of your issues to the relevant Confluence page where that work will be created. Obviously, our team uses Confluence to create our work, and I recommend that agile marketing teams that use Jira Software also use Confluence. In order to implement Confluence properly, you need to understand key concepts.

Here are the main concepts of Confluence you need to know.

Spaces

Confluence has this concept called a space. A space is a place in which a certain type of work is done. You could have a space for a department, like marketing. And all of marketing's work is created in this space. Another approach, which I think is an excellent approach, is to create a Confluence space for every Jira Software project. This way, you have alignment between where work is tracked and where work is created. You can also keep permissions aligned. Let's say you have a private project in Jira to track work with a vendor. You can have a space in Confluence and restrict access to the same people for both the Jira project and the Confluence space.

Permissions

Confluence has sophisticated permissions just like Jira, so you can set up Confluence to do anything from making all of your pages and spaces open to anyone in the company to create, edit, comment, and delete content to making spaces completely private and not even viewable by anyone else in Confluence except for the people in the space. And anything in between.

You could have one marketing space that is more open. And you could use this space to create content for your projects, collaborate with others in the organization on that content, and share what you are working on with the entire organization.

You could set up a second marketing space called "Marketing Leaders" And only have your marketing leadership in it and make this space only viewable to your marketing team. This way you can create and collaborate on ideas in private as a team.

You can also create a space that has content on it that is useful to everyone else in the company. For example, you create a "Marketing Processes" space to show your checklists and processes for how to work with marketing. You could publish your style guide and branding guidelines, you could publish the procedure for requesting business cards or requesting schwag for a field event.

Once these procedures are written and published in your Confluence space, you can integrate that with your Jira Service Desk (see next section) and when people request these things from you, the page will automatically show up to help them do it themselves. They might even save you from taking that request in the first place. Less work for you.

This is just one example of how your marketing team can use a space.

Templates

To make creating content easier, you can create templates in Confluence so that when you create a new page, a template shows up and only needs to be modified. Marketing templates could include:

- Brochure for booth at a conference
- Blog post
- White paper
- Press release or media alert
- Go-to-market plan
- Facebook ad set
- Webinar landing page description
- Meeting agenda, notes
- Sprint retrospective
- Sprint review

You can certainly think of other work you do that has a similar format each time you do it. Templates in Confluence could make your life much, much easier.

Searchable by entire team

A typical thing most marketing teams do is create content, processes, checklists, and meeting notes in Microsoft Office or Google Docs, or a similar document creation product. There is nothing wrong with that, except when you need to go find something. These tools have a paradigm of owners and folders. Documents are difficult to share and find. Think about it. How easy is it to find that press release from last May? How easy is it for other people on the team to find it? If someone else created the press release and did not share it with me, I cannot find it.

Confluence is different because it is designed to be a wiki with a web page paradigm, not a folder and creator paradigm. Even though that page is created by someone, that page is not really owned by the creator. It is the property of the space. So, anyone in the space can find it or have equal access to it as anyone else. You can restrict access to pages in a space, but in general, if you create a team space, you want the team to have access to the content. What you create is findable by the entire team. You can always search the space or go through the page navigation on the left side of Confluence to find that press release from May.

Communicate and collaborate with the rest of the organization

Confluence is not just about creating documents. It is about communicating and collaborating with the rest of the organization. If you set up your marketing Confluence space the way you should, you can make all or most of your work available to everyone in your company (or at least the right stakeholders). When you create a go-to-market plan for a new product launch, others can provide input while you are working on the plan. Even in the first draft, you can notify others that the page is started. Every time the page gets updated, people get a notification. This pulls people into your document prompting them to contribute early.

The worst thing you can do is create a complete go-to-market plan until you get to a final draft stage and then share it. That is not agile. You may go through all that work and be wrong. Or miss important points. An agile marketing team involved stakeholders and customers early on in the process of work, collected feedback, and addresses feedback throughout the process of developing work. You should share your first and early drafts with anyone and everyone, to get them to contribute early and often, so you don't get too off track.

If you ask people for ideas, they have no idea. But if you give people ideas in the form of early drafts, it gives people something to poke holes at so you can refine it. That is a much more effective way to work. You just have to put your ego in check and internalize the belief that first drafts and first ideas usually stink. If you can do that, it's easier to start working on something, share it early, and get input so you can revise and make it better faster.

Integration with Jira Service Desk for self-service

One of the coolest Confluence features is that it integrates with Jira Service Desk. We will get to Jira Service Desk in the next section, but for now, understand this. Do you answer the same questions over and over again, like, "How do I get the official logo to use in my presentation?" or "Where can I find the presentation template?" I bet you do. I am sure you'd like a place where these instructions live and that people can find them and answer these questions themselves.

You can create pages that answer these questions and put them on your Confluence page. That way you can just send people a link to the page or remind people to search for it. You can even create a page in Confluence called "How to get help from marketing" and provide links to all pages describing these procedures.

You can integrate these pages with your Jira Service Desk, so that when people go to your request forms and start to type in the subject line for their request, the keywords they use will automatically find and then display the procedure pages right on the page next to the form they are filling out. Your stakeholder will see this and maybe not even complete the form. They will say "Wow. Look at that. An article that says, *How to get the official company logo for presentations.* I'll just click on that."

Confluence is where you create work and collaborate around that work. Jira Software is where you plan and track that work. Not all of our work is planned. There are times when we need to respond to requests, answer questions, and otherwise provide support to the rest of our organizations. Most marketing teams either just receive emails individually or create a shared email inbox called "marketing@yourcompany. com" to receive and respond to these requests. The problem with the email inbox solution is that there is no accountability, and there is no visibility into the service you provide. This is where Jira Service Desk comes into play.

Jira Service Desk

Strictly speaking, you will not use Jira Service Desk to run scrum or kanban on your marketing team. You will use Jira Software for that. So now you must be thinking, "Then why are we talking about Jira Service Desk?" Here's why. Agile marketing is to help you with planned work. To be proactive about taking on important projects, breaking them down into small pieces, delivering on these projects in small bits, gathering feedback along the way and improving as you go. But as you know, not all of our work is planned.

Some of our work is unplanned and reactive. Some of our work is responsive to requests from people all over our organization: requests for business cards, brochures, templates, reports, etc. These urgent requests often interrupt us and prevent us from spending time on our important (planned) work. I'm not saying we completely ignore the urgent unplanned work. I am saying we need a process for handling them, so they don't take over our lives. I am suggesting you use Jira Service Desk to set up a process so that all employees can make requests of marketing through forms you create and so you can track and respond transparently to these requests.

What to know about Jira Service Desk

Although you will not use Jira Service Desk to implement agile marketing, I recommend you use it to handle your unplanned work, so you can focus more effectively on your planned work. At the end of this book, in the implementation plan, I suggest adding Jira Service Desk after you are comfortable with agile marketing in Jira Software and Confluence. Once you build that habit, then get Jira Service Desk going.

In this section, I will discuss how Jira Service Desk works, so you know what is possible. But later in the book, when I start to describe specifically how we set up Jira Software and Confluence to run kanban and scrum, I will not go into the details about how we implement Jira Service Desk. By learning Jira Service Desk concepts in this section, you will understand plenty about how we use it and how you will use it. For now, let's talk about what Jira Service Desk can do.

Jira Service Desk concepts

Jira Service Desk has the following concepts:

- Web portal and forms
- Queues
- Service level agreements
- Reports
- Roles: agents and customers
- Integration with Confluence for self-service

Let's talk about each.

Web portal and forms

For starters, Jira Service Desk allows you to create a web portal with forms on it that you can publish on your (Confluence) intranet or on your website. You can use Jira Service Desk for employees or for customers or both. For purposes of this discussion, we will stick to serving employees, not customers.

The idea is that you create a set of forms so that you can take specific requests from employees throughout your organization. Think about all of the emails you receive from people in your organization. You can create a form for each of these and be very specific about what is on the form. An example form might be for a business card request. You might have the following fields on the "Business Card Request Form:

- Name (as you want it to appear on the card):
- Title:
- Address:
- Phone number:
- Email:
- Linkedin URL:

- Twitter URL:
- Due Date:
- Comments:

Jira Service Desk is great because you can customize the forms. You can make the forms as specific or as generic as you want. For example, your business card request form could be nothing more than:

- Subject
- Description
- Due Date

Then you could provide an explanation for what to put next to each field. For example, next to the description field, you could display text like this.

"In the description field, provide your name, title, address, phone number, and email address."

The point here is that you can customize what the form is, so you have very specific forms for each type of request people make or you can have one form for everything. Although it will not happen overnight, because change is hard, you really can set up a Jira Service Desk portal and eliminate all the emails that people send you to ask for things. You just send people to your portal.

Queues

Once these forms are submitted, each request can be placed in a queue. Only your marketing team has access to the queues, and you can set up any queues you want. Queues have two advantages. First, you can divide up the work. Each queue collects a certain type of request. Business card requests in one queue and event support requests in another. You could also create queues that show requests that have not been responded to within 24 hours. This is a way to call attention to requests the team has not worked on yet.

Second, you can have multiple people working certain queues. If issues are placed in a queue, then if one person is out for the day, another member of the marketing team can go into the queues and easily start working on requests. Issues don't get lost or forgotten or ignored.

Why use queues? Jira Software is designed so that an issue has one assignee. One person owns the work for an issue and only one person can be assigned an issue. For most work, this is the way it should be. One person should be responsible for a task. One person should own it. This philosophy does not work in a service management environment. What if someone is on vacation or calls in sick? Issues assigned to that person will not get done that day or that week. That's a problem.

In Jira Service Desk, issues are put in a queue, and a team of people can go into the queue and "pick up" an issue, assign it to themselves, and start working on it. If that person is out for a day, after they have "picked-up" an issue and has not yet resolved it, anyone else on the team can go through the queue that day and see what is being worked on, what is not done yet, and then "pick up" the issues from others and continue to work them. Queues are a great way to change the culture of your marketing team to be service-oriented.

Service level agreements

When you set up Jira Service Desk, you imply to the rest of your organization that you are going to provide a certain level of service. This puts pressure on your team. It also sets expectations that requests will be replied to in a certain amount of time. You can set these expectations with service level agreements (SLAs). Jira Service Desk allows you to set SLAs, and there are two main types: time to first response and time to resolution.

Time to first response: The time it takes from the moment an employee makes a request to the moment someone on your team responds. This could be something as simple as responding: "Hi, I have your request, and I will work on it soon and get back to you." This does not mean you will work on it right away. Maybe it will still take you three days to resolve this particular request. Maybe longer. Time to first response is an SLA that is about being responsive. This is a good SLA to have when there is a lot of uncertainty in how long it will take you to help people with their requests.

Time to resolution: The time it takes from the moment an employee makes a request to the moment the request is resolved or otherwise closed and completed.

With these two SLA metrics, your marketing team can now use Jira Service Desk to set up service processes and make promises to your "customers" about the service they will receive. You will be able to measure your success and know when you are living up to your promises.

Reports

Jira Service Desk allows you to monitor how you are doing. You can report on how many requests you receive and by what time, how long each request takes, who on your team is doing which types of requests or how many requests they do. You can report on how many requests get resolved on time and how many do not. The point is, you can start to actually measure how effective your teams is at delivering service to the rest of the company. You cannot do that with a shared email inbox.

Roles: Agents and customers

There are two types of roles on Jira Service Desk that are relevant to your team. An agent is someone on your team who has access to the queues, forms, SLAs, and reports in Jira Service Desk. Agents can respond to requests and create queues, SLAs, and reports. The agent role also matters because Atlassian charges for Jira Service Desk based on the number of agents you have. If you have a marketing team of ten people, you would likely assign only three people on your team to be agents and only pay for those three accounts.

The other role to understand is the customer role. The customer is all of your employees who get access to the web portal and the forms. You do not pay for customers in Jira Service Desk. They are free. So, if you are a marketing team of ten people in a company of one thousand employees, you can have 990 employees using your portal for free. Not a bad deal. Remember, in Jira Service Desk, you pay for agents, not customers.

Integration with Confluence for self-service

As we discussed in the section on Confluence, you can integrate Jira Service Desk and Confluence. You do this in order to improve self-service for employees. The integration works well because when an employee is filling out one of your forms, Jira Service Desk detects the keywords typed into the form, and while the employee is still typing, it searches your Confluence space for pages related to the request and displays snippets of those pages on the form. It happens in real time so that an employee could see answers to their question before they complete the form. This is great because some employees will see the article and instead of completing the form, they will click over to the page and solve their own problem. Wouldn't you like more of your employees to be a little more self-sufficient?

To give you an example of how it works, consider an employee making a request for your company logo. The employee types this phrase into the subject line of your collateral request form:

"I need a vector file of our logo"

While the employee is typing this phrase, a Confluence page containing those keywords shows up on the page, next to the form, with a headline of the page:

"Where to find a vector file of the company logo."

It is quite incredible to see it happen in real time. And because the list of relevant articles appears while the employee is filling out the form, they will visually be drawn to look at the movement on the page, and say to themselves, "Huh, that might be exactly what I need." Then click through to the Confluence page.

Let's review

The tools we use on our marketing team are Jira Software, Confluence, and Jira Service Desk. Now that you understand what each of these tools can do, the rest of this book will be highly understandable, and dare I say, entertaining, as I walk through how we actually set up our tools for how we work.

As you read the rest of this book, I want you to think about two things in the back of your mind. First, because the Atlassian tools are highly configurable, you will get a picture of how we set them up for us. Based on your current understanding of the concepts of Jira and Confluence, you might ask yourself, "Why did they set it up that way? Why didn't they set it up this other way? That is how I would set it up. I wonder if I can set it up that way?" These are the right questions to ask. I do not describe how we set up Jira and Confluence to tell you how you should do it, but how we did it. How you set these tools up is almost limitless, and you should set them up to suit your needs. Learn from how we did it. As you do, write down ideas for how you want to do it.

The second thing I want you to think about as you read this book is how imperfectly we implemented agile marketing and set up Jira and Confluence. We did not go for perfection. We went for starting. And learning. And making improvements as we learned. We made the assumption that we would not get it right at the beginning. I am very open about the mistakes we made to demonstrate this point. I have an entire chapter about our mistakes. I urge you to take a similar approach. Get started. Learn. Improve.

5. How We Set Up Scrum in Jira

"Start by doing what's necessary; then do what's possible; and suddenly you are doing the impossible."

~ Francis of Assisi

This is the part of the book where you get to look under the hood and get a glimpse at how we set up Jira Software to run scrum. I will walk you through each major part of our configuration and why we made the decisions we made. I will hold very little back. I want you to learn from our experience.

Here we go.

Project types and projects

It all begins with project types. We have three types of projects:

One for each line of business: To give you one example, one of our lines of business is our Atlassian consulting practice. We have a project in Jira called "Atlassian." We keep track of all marketing work related to this line of business in the

Atlassian project. That could be writing white papers, paid media campaigns, webinars, and the podcast.

One for each major project that has a finite life span: A traditional definition of a project requires that the project has an end date. When there is a big project that we know will have an end date, but is complicated enough to have its own workspace, we create a project in Jira. One example of this would be a website redesign project. The last time we redesigned our website, we created a stand-alone project in Jira called "Website Redesign." We planned and tracked all of that work in that project. One other example is when we sponsor a major conference. We sponsor two major conference per year. Atlassian Summit and Gainsight Pulse. For each, we created a project.

One for each other major type of work that is ongoing and big enough to break out from the line of business projects or for types of work that span across lines of business: For this project type, it is a judgement call. For our podcast, Helping Sells Radio, we created a stand-alone project. We wanted to keep this work separate from other projects because of the ongoing nature of the show. There were launch tasks that ended after we launched. Now there is the ongoing work of planning, recording, delivering, and promoting each show.

There is no one way to create projects. It is a judgement call. You should create a project when:

- The work is big enough, separate enough from other types of work, and has a definite end date.
- You will, today or may one day, want only a certain number of people working on a project. In other words, when you want to set permissions so only

a certain group of people have access. A project for work with an agency, for example.

- You want ease of reporting project activity.

One last piece of advice. Don't create a project for everything. Soon, your project list will grow to such a length, that you will start asking yourself, "Where should this task go? In the event project or the promotion project? Or maybe it should go in the social media project?"

Don't overdo it.

Permission schemes: Defining who has access and to what

We have a fairly open permission scheme set up. With very few exceptions, all members of the team have access to all projects. Team members have permissions to create, change, and delete issues. That may be too open for you. Permissions can be configured to do a lot, down to preventing people from deleting issues and changing due dates. So, you can lock down permissions. We chose not to go this route in the interest of reducing friction. We are a small enough team, with high enough trust that we don't feel the need to do that.

However, if you want more control over what people can see and do, Jira allows you to do that. You can set up permissions such that certain projects are not visible to certain people (or groups). You could provide view only access. You can also set permissions so that people can add issues and comments but not delete issues.

In a few cases, we have contractors or agencies helping us on projects. We provide those people access to the Jira project within which they are working and only that project. When these people log in to Jira, they only see work being performed in that project and will have no visibility into other Jira activity.

Issue types

When we set up Jira, we created dozens of issue types. We asked each person on the team, "What type of work do you do and how to you want to plan and track that work?" We came up with a rather long list of issue types that looked something like this:

- Webinars
- Ad campaigns
- Events
- Graphic design
- Content
- Sales enablement
- Branding
- Customer stories
- Podcast
- Schwag requests
- Website redesign
- Product marketing
- Content

The list goes on.

When you create an issue type, you get to decide what fields are on it. These are the fields we had on our webinar issue type:

- Summary
- Description
- Assignee
- Reporter
- Guest speaker
- Webinar date
- Due date

- Sprint
- Epic link
- Story points

Each time we created a new webinar issue, which we usually did the moment we had a webinar idea, we filled in each of these fields. Most of these fields are self-evident but let me explain each one briefly and why we created it.

Summary: This is the issue subject line. Here we wrote the topic of the webinar or the working title.

Description: This is an open text field on which we wrote a brief description of what the webinar would be about and the key objectives of the webinar. The information types here formed the basis for what would be written on the landing page.

Assignee: The person who owned the webinar delivery.

Reporter: The person who created the webinar issue. So, I would create the issue, then "assign" it to someone else on the team.

Guest speaker: Most of our webinars involve a main guest speaker who is not a ServiceRocket employee. So, we captured the speaker's name here.

Webinar date: Date when the webinar would be delivered.

Due date: Date when the webinar project would be completed. This date took into account post-webinar tasks like sending follow-up emails and uploading the recording to the landing page.

Sprint: In the sprint field, we indicate what sprint this issue should be completed in. During sprint planning, which we talk about later in the book, the team decides which issues will be done in a sprint. When that happens, you "mark" each issue with the name of the sprint, using this field.

Story points: For estimating the workload of the issue.

By reading this list, you can imagine what fields you would

put on your webinar issue type. Actually, as I write this section, I can think of other fields I'd like to add and remove. If you go back to the list of our issue types above, you can also imagine that each issue type had its own set of fields.

Creating your issue types

When you start creating your issue types, think about what the fields will be for each. There is no right way to do it other than to say, you should customize the minimum amount possible so that your team can easily distinguish between work types without creating unnecessary customizations that need to be managed. We started off over-customizing (one of the mistakes we made) and then had to roll it back because things got way too complicated. Let's just take the webinar issue type as an example. The more we did webinars, the less we filled in all the fields. When we wrote the name of the guest speaker in the description, there wasn't much need to type the name again in the guest speaker field. Sometimes, we would not know who the guest speaker would be until much of the planning had been completed.

Before you start creating issue types in Jira, make a list of all the issue types you think you might want. Then try to consolidate as many as you can and try not to create too many.

Jira Software does come with standard issue types and you can use those. The problem is that they will be too generic for you and they will look too much like issue types for software teams. For example, one Jira Software issue type is called "bug." No marketing team wants that. Although, now that I type that, if you are managing your company website, you might want to use the bug issue type.

The lesson here is that even though I say you don't want to create too many custom issue types or over-customize your issue types, you should create and use issue types unique to how you work. If there is one standard issue type that you should use and not customize, it is the epic issue type. All agile marketing teams using scrum, need to use the epic issue type.

The epic issue type

An epic is a major task that will be completed over more than one sprint. A project generally has multiple epics and within those epics, there are multiple tasks and subtasks. Here is an example.

Let's say you are planning an event. The event is big enough that you created a project for it. Within that project you will have a few major types for work.

1. Planning the event
2. Promoting the event
3. Running the event
4. Post event activities

If the event is three months away, and you are doing two-week sprints, you will complete this event project in six sprints. Looking at the list of tasks above, ask yourself, "Will we complete any of these tasks in a single two-week sprint?" For example, will you "promote the event" in a two-week period? Probably not. Think of all the tasks associated with promoting an event:

- Create the promotion plan
- Get budget approval
- Create and run the email campaign
- Create and run the social media campaign
- Personally invite influencers to share it

Since you know you will promote the event over four to eight weeks, you need to break that up and spread your promotion plan over several sprints. To do this in Jira, you create an epic issue type and call it "Event Promotion." Then, you create a task for each item you need to plan, create, and run promotions for the event.

Every time you run a sprint planning meeting, you will take some of the event promotion tasks and add them to the current sprint. You would do this for each of your epics, so that in each sprint, you plan a certain part of that promotion plan until the promotion plan is completed.

We just got into the weeds a bit, and we will spend more time on the process of using the epic issue type, but for now, I want you to understand that no matter what issue types you create or how you customize them, you will need to use the standard Jira epic issue type. You will need it to run scrum properly.

Enough about issue types, let's talk about how we set up workflows.

Our workflows

At first, we went a little crazy setting up our workflows. Over time, we simplified our workflows from having over a dozen different workflows with an average of 5.8 steps to six workflows and an average of 4.8 steps. Much more manageable.

This is a list of our workflows.

- 3 Status Workflow - 3 steps
- Global 4-Step Workflow - 4 steps
- Newsletter Workflow - 5 steps
- Podcast Workflow - 6 steps
- Service Desk Simple Workflow - 5 steps
- Webinar Workflow - 6 steps

In the real world of our scrum process in Jira, the global 4-step workflow covers 90% of our projects. We still use the podcast workflow because of the work we put into automating the creation of sub-tasks at each workflow step, but other than that, we primarily use the global 4-step workflow.

The service desk simple workflow does not apply to our scrum processes because the work that comes through the service desk is unplanned work handled by our marketing operations team.

I would like to show you how two of our workflows look to give you an idea of how we actually set up our workflows. Let's start with the global 4-step workflow.

Global 4-step workflow

As the name implies, there are 4 steps in this workflow. Those steps are as follows:

1. Open
2. In Progress
3. In Review
4. Closed

Simple as that.

Podcast workflow

When I said we went a little crazy with our workflows, this podcast workflow demonstrates that. It is also a thing of beauty. Our podcast workflow looks like this:

- Open
- Plan
- Execute

- Publish
- Promote
- Closed

There are six steps in this workflow and each step reflects reality. When we have an idea for a podcast, we create a podcast issue type and leave it in "open" status. Once we know we are going to do that podcast episode, we click on "plan" to move the task into that status. This is where things get interesting with this workflow. We added some automation.

At each stage of this podcast workflow, there are several sub-tasks that we complete every time. For example, at the plan step, we do the following things:

- Book the guest and get it on the calendar
- Create the show notes on a Confluence page
- Research guest/topic
- Add questions to the shows notes page

I don't know about you, but I don't want to create sub-tasks and type up the descriptions every time we do a podcast. And then to have to do this for each workflow step which might have four of five sub-tasks each? That's approximately 30 sub-tasks just to run a podcast. We used an app called Scriptrunner, by a company called Adaptivist, to automate the creation of these sub-tasks. Whenever we click on the "plan" workflow button, all four of those sub-tasks are created automatically and assigned to the person who originally created the podcast issue. Not bad, right?

We have the same automation for each workflow step. Obviously, each of the other workflow steps, automatically creates a different set of sub-tasks, related specifically to that workflow step.

The downside to automation and sub-tasks

Automation like this can save you a lot of time and minimize forgetting to do tasks. These are two major benefits, especially when you have tasks that you repeat over and over. There is a downside. Two, actually. First, the best laid plans of mice and men often go awry. After you create these workflow steps, automate all of the sub-tasks, and start working on your tasks (in this case, start running a podcast), you will discover some of the sub-tasks are not quite right. You might find you have unnecessary sub-tasks. For example, we have a sub-task for scheduling a guest and another sub-task to send the calendar invite. These seem reasonable to have and both tasks need to be done, but when you use Calendly to book guests, calendar invites are automatically sent. We don't need two sub-tasks anymore. We need to change the rules in Scriptrunner or live with having an extra sub-task created that we have to close out every time we run a podcast. My point is this. Automation is great, but you cannot set-it-and-forget-it. You will regularly need to tweak your automation rules as you learn and as things change.

The second downside to automation and sub-tasks lies specifically with sub-tasks. Sub-tasks do not play well with scrum. When your team gets to the end of a sprint, and you are doing your sprint retrospective, you end the sprint in Jira. The problem is that you cannot end a sprint when there are open sub-tasks in the sprint. Naturally, you are thinking, "Why would I have open-sub-tasks at the end of the sprint?" If you plan a sprint properly, you won't. However, when you automate the creation of a list of sub-tasks, you may not be able to finish all of your sub-tasks in a sprint no matter what you do. You are planning to fail. Here's why.

You cannot add sub-tasks to a sprint. You can only add tasks. In the case of our podcast issue type, when we plan a sprint, we know going into the sprint that we will not complete all 30 sub-tasks for that episode. From idea to booking a guest to promoting a published show, it could take two or three or four sprints. When we add the podcast tasks to a sprint and click on the next workflow step and then the next, all of those sub-tasks get automatically created. Now we could have a dozen sub-tasks in the sprint that we know we will not work on until the next sprint. Not only does this clutter up the sprint board, but we have planned to not complete all of the work for that sprint. That is no way to plan sprints.

The solution to this problem is to make the podcast issue type an epic, not a task. Then change all of the sub-tasks to tasks. That way, we can add each of those sub-tasks (now a task) to each sprint only when we know we will work on them. We have not done this yet because we have not figured out how to automate the creation of tasks in an epic. We solved this problem by excluding podcast work from our scrum process. Our podcast has its own project, and we set up a separate kanban board in the project to track the work. It is working well for us.

I tell that story to demonstrate that the art of agile marketing is in the imperfections and trade-offs of configuring Jira to how you want to work. As flexible as Jira is, it cannot do everything you want, in the precise manner in which you want to do it. I want you to learn from stories like this and anticipate these little annoyances and trade-offs and work-arounds.

To customize or not to customize workflows

I just showed you two examples of how we created workflows. When we started, we created a lot of custom workflows like our podcast workflow. Over time, we realized that for most work, the workflow was not as unique and special as we originally thought. Having too many steps for most work became cumbersome, and it often felt like way too much time clicking workflow buttons and closing redundant tasks. This led us to simplifying our workflows and using our global 4-step workflow for most of our work.

How we set up our scrum board

The heart of scrum is the board. It helps a team visualize its work. After you set up your projects, permissions, issue types, and workflows, you will create your board. To help you do that, I will show you how we created ours.

Projects we included in our board

One decision to make when setting up your board is what projects will show up on your board. When a project is excluded from a board, you cannot add issues to sprints on that board. You may have projects that you don't want to include in your scrum process, and you can decide not to show those projects on your board. One example is your Jira Service Desk project. These are generally unplanned work requests and should not be included on your scrum board. We excluded our Jira Service Desk project and our podcast project for reasons I described earlier.

Columns

The next choice you will make when setting up your scrum board is how you lay out your columns. Columns are what makes a board visual. We created four columns:

1. To Do
2. In Progress
3. In Review
4. Done

Although your columns should align with your workflows, each project could have its own workflow. If you recall from earlier in this chapter, we created a global workflow with the following stages:

- Open
- In Progress
- In Review
- Closed

Notice there are the same number of columns as there are steps in the global workflow. Although your workflow and columns can differ, you do need to map them so they align. Notice the differences. One column is called "To Do" and one workflow step is called "Open." These are effectively the same thing. We probably should call them the same since we now use a global workflow. In the interest of simplicity, you should map columns and workflow steps and keep them the same. If you want projects to have different/customized workflows, just make sure the number of stages in your workflow is matched to your columns.

Why? So that when you drag an issue from "To Do" into the "In Progress" column, Jira automatically moves the status of the workflow from "Open" to "In Progress."

Swimlanes

A swimlane is a row on the scrum board. In that row, you can display any set of issues you want. For example, you could have a row for each marketing team. You create a swimlane for your marketing operations team and show all the issues for that sprint for the operations team. You could create another swimlane for content marketing. Another for event marketing. Swimlanes make it easy to scroll down your sprint and see issues grouped together by type.

We have swimlanes for each person on the team. When we do our daily stand up, we go around the meeting person by person so it makes sense for us to have a swimlane for each person. We can easily scroll down to my name "Bill" on the board when it is my turn to update the team on the tasks I am working on now or have just completed.

To set up swimlanes, you need to know a little JQL (Jira query language). In our case, we have a swimlane with this JQL for each person.

JQL command: assignee = firstname.lastname

We do this for each member of the team.

Simple as that.

We also like to divide up our work by line of business and by project. So, we could create swimlanes for each line of business and for each project. It would be great to divide up our board and have a swimlane for each line of business or project. That would look like this:

A swimlane for each line of business:
- JQL command: project = lineofbusinessA
- JQL command: project = lineofbusinessB
- JQL command: project = lineofbusinessC

A swimlane for each project:
- JQL command: project = WebRedesign
- JQL command: project = AtlassianSummit(Event)

If you really want to get fancy with swimlanes, you could create one to display issues in rows by due date. Let's say you want to display issues in your board by when they are due. You could create a series of swimlanes to create rows like this.

You could have a swimlane for each of the following:

- Issues due yesterday
- Issues due today
- Issues due tomorrow
- Issues due rest of the sprint

We don't do it this way, but as I write this, I think we might want to try this. This could be especially useful in daily scrum meetings when answering the three questions:

1. What did you do to advance the sprint yesterday?
2. What will you do to advance the sprint today?
3. What is getting in your way?

When you address the first question in the meeting, you could have the swimlane on the screen showing all the issues that were due yesterday and see clearly the status of everything the team needed to complete by the previous day. This brings the team together around all the issues. This discussion would have a very different feel than going through the meeting getting an update person-by-person.

You never get the perfect Jira set up

If there is anything difficult about Jira, it is knowing all that is possible. I have been using Jira daily since mid-2013, and I still think about ideas like this for how to use it. This is an example of how Jira can grow with your team and evolve with how your team works. In just this small example, you see a team that is used to scrolling through swimlanes by person and asking each person in a daily stand up meeting to give an update. A team like this could get off track because the meetings become about the person and not about the issue or the agreed upon due date. Maybe the stand up drifts into talking about things people are working on that are not in the sprint. "I have a meeting today with Eva to talk about next steps in the webinar we are planning." Instead of, "Yesterday, I completed issue AT-123 to publishing the landing page for the webinar in March."

By simply changing the swimlane configuration to create a row by due date, we can switch the nature of the stand up from a focus on people and their work to the work and the due dates (or otherwise, changing the focus of the stand up to be in the moment about the work we need to do today to advance the sprint).

This is just an example. The point is, you can be very creative about how you configure Jira in any of these areas. Jira can be configured to reflect how you work OR you can configure Jira to influence how you work.

Quick filters

Whereas swimlanes help you divide up the issues on your board by rows, a quick filter allows you to display only certain issues on the board. This removes the clutter and the need to scroll down your entire board to view each row.

One of the most useful functions in Jira, especially for scrum, is the quick filter. As you start getting into scrum, you will find that the number of issues in the backlog becomes overwhelming. You could have hundreds or even thousands of tasks in your backlog. When you do backlog grooming or sprint planning, it can become prohibitive to go through the list of issues and make sense of it. You need a way to filter out only the issues you want to see for the specific conversation you are having at the time.

For example, let's say that you are in a sprint planning meeting and are deciding as a team what issues to work on for the upcoming event you have planned next month. With one month to go, you certainly have tasks you need to get done in the next two weeks. Maybe it is to finalize the creatives for signage, brochures, and handouts. Maybe it is to get the first draft of presentation slides from the speakers. Or maybe there are some tasks that you cannot think of right now, that you need to get done in the next two weeks.

When you look at your backlog in Jira, let's say there are 798 total issues listed. How are you going to find the few related tasks for this event you are planning? You can do this with a quick filter. A quick filter uses the fields in Jira to only show you the issues you want to see on the screen. In this case, you could create a quick filter that shows only issues in the event project that are not completed and are labeled for your primary product line. This is just one example, but if you create a quick filter like this in Jira, you can go to your backlog of 798 issues, click on the quick filter called "Product Line X Events" at the top of the backlog, to see only issues with those parameters. Now you only see 14 issues on your backlog. Much better. We can look at those issues only and make decisions on which we should get done in the next sprint.

Quick filters are an excellent way to remove distractions and improve focus during sprint planning.

What our quick filters look like

Quick filters show up as links at the top of your board by name. You can click on each link to show only the issues for that quick filter. We have three kinds of quick filters.

1. Quick filters for each line of business
2. Quick filters for each person on the team
3. Quick filters for odds and ends like "unassigned issues, recently updated issues, and open issues, and epics"

Below are a few examples of JQL for our quick filters.

Quick filters for each line of business look like this:

    JQL command: project = lineofbusinessA

    JQL command: project = lineofbusinessB

Quick filters for each person looks like this:

    JQL command: assignee = bill.cushard

    JQL command: assignee = firstname.lastname

Quick filter for unassigned issues looks like this:

    JQL command: assignee is empty

We primarily use quick filters during sprint planning meetings to narrow down the topic we are discussing at any one time during the planning. For example, when we want to focus our planning on one single line of business, we click on the quick filters for line of business one, and then talk about what work we want to get done for that line of business in that sprint. By displaying only tasks for that line of business during that discussion, we focus all our energies on that. This process helps us identify what issues need to get done and what issues have not yet been created that we need to create and then move into that sprint.

As with swimlanes, you will use a little JQL to create your quick filters.

Card colors

As you look at a board for your active sprint, issues can blend together visually. Swimlanes and quick filters help you visually focus on certain issues by certain categories. You can further categorize your issues with colors. Jira lets you assign colors to your issues using all the usual categories. You could assign a color based on any parameter using JQL like we did for swimlanes and quick filters. And your brand marketers will be happy to know that you can use your branding style colors down to the RGB and hexadecimal codes.

One interesting way to use colors is by due date. You could assign a color of green for issues not due until next week. Assign orange to issues due in the next three days. Assign red to issues that are overdue. You could assign colors by person, by team, by step in the work (show purple for all issues that are "in review"). These are just a few examples. We keep it simple and assign a color for each line of business.

Card layout

When you look at a card on your board, what do you want to see besides color? The name of the issue? The due date? Who it is assigned to? Yes. All of these, probably. Maybe a few more things. Keep in mind, the card on a board in Jira is pretty small. So, you want to display the minimum amount of data, but enough so that you know what the issue is all about. The good news is that Jira limits you to displaying only three extra items on a card.

For cards on the backlog you can view:

- Created (date)
- Issue type
- Assignee

For cards displayed on an active sprint you can view:

- Due date
- Issue type
- Assignee

Estimation

Estimating work is an important part of scrum. Only by estimating your team's work, can you understand how much work your team can commit to during a sprint. Estimating is the only way to know how much additional work you can take on or swap out when new work is presented to your team during a sprint.

As you will learn later in this book, we do not use estimating in our scrum process. Yes, certified scrum masters and agile coaches may now criticize us. I can take it. We don't estimate, and I explain why we don't later in this book. We should estimate, but we don't. For now, just know that in Jira, you can set up estimating in a variety of different ways, from using story points to time tracking.

Working days

Working days is important because it defines what days of the week should be counted in a sprint. If your sprint is two weeks, do you want that to be 10 business days or 14 calendar days. You can choose to count all seven days of the week or business days Monday through Friday. We choose the latter.

You can also choose "non-working days," which in practical use is your holiday schedule. We add dates to cover the holidays we observe in the United States and Chile since we have people on our marketing team in both countries.

Issue detail view

The issue detail view is a preview of an issue when you click on a card while on the board. When you click on an issue, a preview pane opens up on the right side of the board showing your issue. You can decide what fields show up on that preview, or issue detail view.

You can click on the issue link and open the entire issue, so that the issue is on your entire screen, but the issue detail view is nice because you don't lose your board view. You can click once on each card, then on the issue detail view, and easily click other cards from the same window. This makes it faster to go through and see details of each issue without leaving the board.

There are four categories of fields you can decide to display on the issue detail view.

- General fields
- Date fields
- People
- Links

These are the fields we have set to show in our issue detail view:

Status: Status shows the current workflow status. Whether the issue is in progress, in review, etc.

Epic: This tells us which epic the issue belongs to. We use epics extensively for projects that will occur over a time period more than a single sprint. For us, an epic is a task that will take more than one sprint to complete.

Due Date: This shows when the issue is due.

Created: This shows when the issue was created.

Updated: This shows the date the last time the issue was updated. Which can be any change to the issue.

Reporter: A reporter is the person who created the issue.

Assignee: The assignee is the person who is currently responsible for doing the work on the issue.

Link Issues: This shows links to any documents or pages relevant to that issue. This could be documents in Confluence, a link to a draft landing page in HubSpot or a link to an Adobe Illustrator file that we have stored in Box.

Should you configure Jira to reflect how you work or influence how you work? An essay

I want to conclude this lengthy chapter with a philosophical discussion about how to set up Jira. There are two broad approaches and both have their place. You can set up Jira to reflect how your team works or to influence how it works.

When a team starts to use Jira, the first instinct is to configure it to match the processes and methods and language of how the team currently works. This makes sense because you want your team to go into Jira, especially early on in your use, and see something familiar. Issue types named for real work people do and workflow steps that reflect how actual work gets done on your team and field names that reflect names of things your team recognizes.

If you implement Jira for a marketing team, and they go in and see the following fields on an issue, do you think that marketing team member will log into Jira ever again?

- Priority
- Resolution
- Affects Version(s)
- Fix Version(s)
- Component(s)
- Environment
- Estimate
- Logged
- Development
- Agile

No. They will not. This list of fields would scare away just about any team other than a software engineering team. Yes. Jira should be set up to reflect how your team works.

On the other hand, if you only configure software to reflect how a team currently works, you will never stretch that team or otherwise help that team improve how they work. At least not in any meaningful way. You must also organize Jira to influence how your team works.

Let's look at two examples:

To reflect

Consider an agile marketing team running a daily scrum. A common daily scrum meeting is mostly about going around the room while each person gives an update on the three questions:

1. What did I do to advance the sprint yesterday?
2. What will I do to advance the sprint today?
3. What is getting in my way?

In this mental model, the meeting is about what each individual person is doing. Even if there is a lot of teamwork going on, the meeting is still about what each person is doing. If a team's meetings are run this way, and many are, that team might have a quick filter for each person on the team. So that when it is someone's turn to go, the scrum master clicks on the quick filter for that person to show that person's issues on the board.

"OK, Kira. What is your update?"

Kira's issues are displayed on the board, and Kira gives her update. This is a good practice, actually, because Kira should focus her update on the issues that are in some sort of "in progress" or recently "completed" status. If Kira wanders and talks about meetings she has scheduled or talks about unplanned, urgent work that is not on the board, the scrum master can intervene and bring Kira back on track.

Since that is how most daily scrums work, this is also how many scrum boards are configured, with an orientation towards the work individuals have assigned to them. This is how Jira can be set up to reflect how a team works.

To influence

What if we have a belief that this "person-orientation" to a daily scrum is too focused on the individual and not enough on the team or on the project itself? What if we want to influence the team towards a new orientation (way of working)? We could change how Jira is configured. And we could do this with a simple change that focuses not on quick filters, but on swimlanes and configure swimlanes on the board to show issues by due date.

Consider the three questions of the daily scrum:

1. What did I do to advance the sprint yesterday?
2. What will I do to advance the sprint today?
3. What is getting in my way?

If we really wanted to focus our discussion on advancing the sprint (the project/work), we could create a swimlane to show issues due yesterday and a swimlane to show issues due today. Then, a third swimlane for all other issues. Your JQL might look like this:

Issues Due Yesterday:
- duedate <= -1d

Issues Due Today:
- duedate = startOfDay()

All Other Issues:

- Use the default rule "Everything Else"

You might be thinking, "How does this influence (or change) how we would run our daily scrum?"

When you show the board during your meeting, the top swimlane will show all issues due yesterday no matter who the issues are assigned to. Ideally, they would all be in the "Done" workflow status, but of course not always. The point is that this swimlane shows all of the issues that "the team" committed to finish yesterday. So, the scrum master can now ask the team, "What did WE do to advance the sprint yesterday?" Now the team can discuss those items and do it as a team.

When that discussion is done, the next question for the team is, "What will WE do to advance the sprint today?" The team then focuses on the issues listed in the second swimlane and discusses what everyone will do to complete those tasks today.

To reflect or influence: That is the question

A simple configuration change in Jira can influence how a team works, and this is the way teams continuously improve. Of course, you will run into resistance to changes like these, however small. That is why you will need the leadership necessary to see, make, and reinforce these changes until new habits are formed.

You may begin your journey with Jira by configuring it to reflect how teams work, but you need to progress to a place in which you can configure it to influence how teams work.

6. How We Set Up Confluence

"Life is really simple, but we insist on making it complicated."

~ Confucius

We use Confluence for two main purposes. Confluence is our company intranet. All employees have access to it, and each department has its own space in Confluence where each can create, collaborate, and document their own work. In the case of the marketing team, there is a space called "Marketing." This is where marketing creates and documents all of the work we do.

The second way we use Confluence is for customer projects. ServiceRocket has a separate Confluence instance on which our services delivery team works on customer projects. We invite customers to participate in that space. When we take on a new customer, we create a space in the name of that customer, add the people who will run that project and add all of the customer contacts involved in that project.

In this space, we create meeting notes, project requirements, schedules, documentation, etc. Customers view, comment, and edit the documents in the space. This real-time content and project collaboration allows customers to feel involved and as if there is no silo. ServiceRocket consultants generally do not work in a vacuum. Work products and project plans are created with the customer (or at least in full view of the customer).

Your marketing team may not have a need to interact with customers in this. I share how we use Confluence with customers to plant the idea about using Confluence to work with people outside of your organization. In the case of a marketing team, this could be contractors, vendors, and agency partners. Just as you can track projects in Jira with your agency partners, you can create and collaborate on content with outside people using Confluence.

In the rest of if this chapter, I will focus on how we use Confluence to run our marketing team, but I wanted you to know what is possible using Confluence with people external to your organization.

Let's return to our marketing space so you can understand how we set it up.

Marketing space home page

If anyone in the company wants to know anything about marketing, they go to our marketing space on our company intranet. Every space in Confluence has a home page. The space home page is a place to communicate what the space is all about. We do four main things on our home page.

Our mission: Display our team mission on the top center of the page.

Who we are: We have a profile picture, name, title, and link to the personal profile page of every member of the team.

How to work/communicate with us: We have buttons that link to three of our most used Jira Service Desk forms. These three buttons are: *Fix a website bug, Have an idea?* and *Something else?* People use these buttons to get to our Jira Service Desk portal and request services from marketing.

List a menu of topics to make it easy to find things: The fourth thing we do on our home page is show navigation links to each main marketing function. These links include our branding guidelines, marketing calendar, campaigns, customer stories, marketing process, and many other marketing functions.

The space home page is the entry point for all things marketing, so we want to make it easy for ServiceRocket employees to find what they need. We also try to design it so that it is easy for our team to find our work. After all, we use our marketing space too.

Space shortcuts

On the top left corner of a space is a navigation menu called "space shortcuts." This is a place for putting links to the most important resources for that space. These links can be linked to other Confluence pages or links to external services.

Our space shortcuts has these six links on it:

1. Marketing Jira
2. Marketing Calendar
3. Editorial Calendar
4. Meeting Notes
5. Projects
6. Retrospectives

Marketing Jira is a link to our Jira, which of course is not in Confluence. All of the other links point to other pages in our marketing space. These links can be changed anytime. In fact, one of the best things about writing this book is discovering new ways to improve how we work. As I write this, I thought of more useful links we could put on our shortcuts list. It also occurred to me that we should rotate these links throughout the year as our priorities shift. For example, leading up to the two major conferences we sponsor, we should have links to our planning documentation for those projects on this space shortcuts list, to name just one example.

Page tree

Just below the space shortcuts is the page tree. This is the main navigation menu for our space, which displays all of the main sub-pages to the space home page. Here is a partial list of the links on our page tree.

- Branding
- Campaigns
- Events
- Content Marketing
- Product Marketing
- Process Library
- Customer Stories
- ServiceRocket Media

Each of these items links to a page in our space. For example, branding links to the page where employees can find the official logos, presentation templates, and our style guide. That is an example of a page we use to communicate to the organization. The branding pages don't change often, but they are used often.

Other pages on this list are used primarily for creating work. Let's take the content marketing menu item and go into some detail about how we use that.

On the content marketing page, there is a link to all the work we do for our blog, including writing the posts.

How we use Confluence to run our blog

With few exceptions, every blog published on our website was written in Confluence. The marketing team writes blogs here, and anyone at ServiceRocket could propose and write a blog here too. We encourage anyone at ServiceRocket to contribute to our blog, especially our experts in consulting and support, who solve interesting challenges for customers. To help reduce friction in the blog creation process, we set up our blog page in Confluence to cover three processes:

How to blog: We have a page that describes how to write a blog, what topics we are looking for, our writing guidelines, and the process for proposing a blog. If someone at ServiceRocket ever has an idea for a blog, we want them to come to this page and then help them write the blog.

Blog template: On the blog page in Confluence, we have a public blog template that employees can use to help write their blog. Not only does the template have a basic outline, it asks for things like the target audience, target product, purpose of the blog, what the call-to-action should be, and a place to list quotes from the blog for social media.

Links to every blog every written: There is a child page called "Blog Posts." This is the page that links to all blogs. When someone creates a new page to write their blog, it is created as a child page to the "Blog Posts" page. On the blog posts page, we have a macro called "Children Display" which automatically adds a link to every child page created for the "Blog Posts" page. This small automation saves time and makes sure all blog posts show up on the blog posts page.

Page organization matters

When we set up our Confluence space, we wanted to make it easy to find things. Our space organization is far from perfect, but there is one thing we do fairly well. Like our blog page, we have structured other pages in a similar way, so that all child pages can be easily found. We do this for webinars, podcasts, events, ebooks, and our process library. All webinar content is created as child pages to the webinars page. All marketing processes are created as child pages to the process library page. This simple organization structure makes it easier to know where to create something new and where to find something that has already been created.

Templates we use

We have already discussed our public blog template. Templates are one of the most useful features in Confluence. You can create any number of templates, so that when someone creates a new page in Confluence, the template design starts the page and can make creating the content easier.

Here is a list of templates we use:

- Public Blog Template
- Customer Story Template
- Go To Market Campaign Checklist
- Webinar
- Event
- Meeting notes: This comes standard in Confluence, and you can edit it.
- Retrospective: This comes standard in Confluence, and I recommend you use it to run all of our sprint retrospective meetings.

Create templates for any work you repeat frequently and that should have some standardization.

Permissions

All ServiceRocket employees have access to our Confluence intranet and to our marketing space. We could set permissions to limit access to our marketing space, but we have an open culture at ServiceRocket. We have set permissions so that all employees can add content and comments in our space wherever they want. The only restrictions we put on non-marketing team employees is that they cannot delete content in our space.

Document processes

We have a process library. This is where we list all of our processes so that the knowledge our team has is not stored only in our heads. Some of these processes are simple checklists. Some of these processes are flow charts. Lucidcharts integrates well with Confluence. Some processes are very detailed and kept up to date. Others lack detail and if you read through the process, you would not be able to repeat it. I share that so you understand our process library is not perfect. It is a work in progress and work sometimes gets in the way of documenting the work, which I admit is not good practice.

However imperfect, here is a short example of processes we have documented. Consider what processes you would document.

- Campaigns
- Paid media
- Webinars
- Podcast
- Go-to-market

This partial list above is an example of work our marketing team produces that repeats over and over. So, we want to document the process. The more we document, the better to can onboard new members of the team. Hiring has been one of the best catalysts for documenting our processes. In 2013, there was no marketing team at ServiceRocket. In 2018, the team is seven, with several freelancers and contractors. Each time we added a new member to the team, we realized how little we had documented. We documented more to make onboarding a little easier on our new team members. We're working on it.

It's time to start working out loud

Confluence is ideal for open, transparent, collaboration work. If you use it with this spirit in mind, it will change how you work. It might even scare you a little. If you use Confluence similarly to how we use it, a lot of people will be able to see you create pages. Confluence users can choose to follow up and get notified when you create a page. When you start a first draft of a new brochure, copy for a product page, or a blog post, people will see it. They can even comment on it.

Are you ready for that? In the spirit of agile marketing, I urge you to embrace it. One of the benefits of an agile approach to work is delivering work to customers earlier in the creation process, collecting feedback, and then making adjustments based on the feedback. The closer to real time you can share your work with your stakeholder, the more agile you will be.

There is no question that making a first draft available to others is scary. But if it makes you feel any better, everyone knows first drafts are awful. So I say, proactively share your first drafts with stakeholders and embrace the feedback. It will make you a better agile marketer.

7. How We Set Up Jira Service Desk

"The best way to find yourself is to lose yourself in the service of others."

~ Mahatma Gandhi

Like you, our marketing team does not work in a vacuum designing marketing campaigns. We spend a reasonable amount of time responding to requests from other parts of the business. When someone on the sales team wants to send a ServiceRocket t-shirt to a customer, they ask us, since we own the t-shirt inventory. If HR is running a recruiting event at a university career expo and wants to bring marketing collateral and schwag, they ask us, since we own the collateral.

In the case of the t-shirt request, we respond to the request saying we will do it and again when it's done. In the case of the career expo, it could turn into a project if we need to create new collateral. We need an organized means for handling these requests. Instead of asking people to "email us with your requests" we use Jira Service Desk.

Marketing as service organization

At ServiceRocket, marketing provides a number of services to employees and teams. Using our Jira Service Desk portal, an employee can:

- Request business cards
- Report problem on the website
- Request schwag
- Offer an idea
- Propose a blog post

Teams can request services from marketing as well.

- The product team can request an ad campaign be run for a product.
- The engineering team can request to publish a blog about a software release (or send an email to customers).
- The sales team can request schwag be sent to customers.
- HR can request a press release for new hires.
- The customer success team can request a customer story be written about a new customer achievement (a testimonial).

We use Jira Service Desk to create a form for each of these requests and then put a link to all of those forms on our marketing space in Confluence, so all employees can find them and make their requests.

We also use Jira Service Desk to communicate status of all requests back to employees. Each employee has the equivalent of an inbox in Jira Service Desk which shows all of their requests.

Employees can see a list of all of their requests, the current status, and all the comments back and forth between a member of our marketing team and them. Employees receive email notifications when a change has been made to the request.

The final benefit of using Jira Service Desk is visibility into requests and our ability to deliver on them. It is very easy to look up requests to see which ones are late or behind schedule and to follow up with the parties involved in the request. The transparency will change how you make service promises because you have the data in Service Desk to back it up.

Jira Service Desk has helped us turn an email box full of random requests that we can never seem to get to, into an organized system for delivering high quality internal service. I am exciting to show you how we set up to inspire you to do the same.

How we set up our Jira Service Desk

First of all, let's talk about how employees get to our Jira Service Desk so they can make their requests. Remember when we talked about our marketing space in Confluence? Our company intranet? There we have links to three of our forms:

1. Fix a Website Bug
2. Have an Idea?
3. Something Else?

When an employee clicks on the button, they are taken to that form on our Jira Service Desk portal.

The portal

We have created a lot of forms broken down into a few categories. Categories make is a bit easier for people to find the form they need. These are our categories:

- Top Requests
- Relations & Community
- Schwag Requests
- Web
- Tools and Application

We have the following forms:

- General Request
- Schwag Request
- Product Collateral Tasks
- Idea
- Event Request
- Graphics Request
- Blog/Content Publication
- Customer Story Request
- Promotion Request
- Public Relations
- Social Media & Communities Task
- New Business Cards
- General Website Request
- Website Fix
- Place an Ad

There is a lot of flexibility in how you make these forms. You can make a form broad and general with just one or two fields that ask:

1. Tell us what you want
2. Tell us why you want it

Or you can be specific and use as many fields as necessary (almost) to collect everything you need for a request. There are trade-offs to each approach. A simple catch-all form may not capture everything you need to fulfill the request because the employee doesn't tell you everything you need to know to help them. A form that is very specific assumes you know what information an employee needs to provide. You might be right, but if you have those specific fields required and the employee doesn't know the information, you turn them away. They might even send you an email instead of filling out your form. You don't want that.

When you design your forms, you should approach it somewhere in the middle. That's what we do.

Warning: When you make request forms available like this. You open up the door to requests. You may get a lot more requests now that you are essentially advertising that you are taking requests. You may not want to do this. On the other hand, aren't you taking these requests anyway? By email? When someone just walks up to your desk? You don't notice it because there isn't a queue. You are probably doing it anyway. With Jira Service Desk, you will notice it. You will be able to track it. You will also then have the data to objectively make decisions about whether to continue to take such requests. You may decide to reduce the services you offer and shut down certain forms. But at least you will be able to make an informed decision.

Queues

Remember, queues are lists in Jira Service Desk where employee requests are stored. We have three types of queues:

A queue for each line of business: Request forms designed for general requests for each line of business show up in this queue. Our marketing team tends to specialize in each line of business. If I am dedicated to line of business A, I will monitor that queue to handle those requests.

A queue for a few high-volume requests: A high-volume request looks like this: schwag requests, business card requests, ideas, marketing tool requests. The queues for these requests is monitored by everyone on the team so that we stay on top of them.

Queues for "I don't know what to call this type of queue" (a.k.a. the catch-all queue): Examples of these queues are: all open tickets, my open tickets, and due soon. The all open tickets queue shows all requests that are still open no matter what request they are. The my open ticket queue shows all open tickets that are assigned to "me." The due soon queue shows all requests due within three days.

These are just examples of the queues we use. You can create different queues. The queues feature has filters that allow you to set the parameters.

Display columns on queues

In a queue, requests will show up in a list and with columns making it easy to see what issues are in the queue and what the issues are about. You can customize what columns are shown, and you can sort each column to put requests in a certain order based on what you care about or what helps you work better.

These are the columns we use:

Key: The ID of the request.
Customer request type: So we know what the request is. A business card request is a customer request type, for example.
Summary: The subject line of the request.
Reporter: The person who make the request.
Assignee: The member of the marketing team to whom the issue is assigned.
Created: When the request was made.

Time to first response: Shows the time it took for someone on the marketing team to respond to the request.

Here is a fresh hot Jira tip: One of the best ways to sort (order) a queue is to sort by the SLA column of your choice. In this case, time to first response. Sort it by ascending. Sorting by ascending time will order the issues in your queue by how close or beyond the service level agreement. By this logic, it means you will prioritize the requests that are over the SLA or close to being over.

This is not perfect, however, because there are times when you might want to work on an issue that just came in even though you have 24 or 48 hours to response (based on the SLA you made with your customers) For example, when your CEO is the reporter. Or when you see an easy one that you know you can just get done in 5 minutes. Just get that one done and move on with your life.

Service level agreements

A service level agreement (SLA) is nothing more than a promise you make to your customers about the quality of service you will provide. In the case of using a tool like Jira that means how long it will take you to do the work that is requested. There are two main service levels you should provide (or promises you should make).

Time to first response: The service level agreement time to first response is just what it sounds like. It is the time it takes from the moment an employee submits a request to the moment you respond to the employee. That's it. Your response might be nothing more than a comment in the request that says, "I have received your request, and I will get to it whenever I darn well please."

It doesn't matter. You met the service level agreement. You responded.

Time to resolution: Time to resolution is a more complete service level agreement because it is the time it takes from the moment an employee submits a request to the moment you close the issues (or otherwise mark the request complete).

There are other service level agreements that we could come up with. But let's stick with these two.

Our team uses time to first response. Not time to resolution. You might think that is the wrong way to do it because if we respond and meet all of our goals, it doesn't mean we actually helped anyone. It is a good point. Just because I am telling you we chose time to first response does not mean you should. It does not mean it is the right way to do it. It just means that is the SLA we chose.

We chose time to resolution for two basic reasons. First, we believe it is very important to be responsive and to get back to people to let them know we have received their request and are working on it. Second, we know we are not going to give everyone what they want. And we know lead times can be long for certain things. If someone requests t-shirts for a recruiting event in three weeks and we have to order more shirts, we don't want to leave the issue open for two to three weeks when a time to resolution SLA would be 48 hours. So we respond quickly, and then we have some freedom to resolve issues quickly or leave them open for as long as necessary.

Reports in Jira Service Desk

By definition, if you implement Jira Service Desk, you are making a promise to your stakeholders about delivering a certain high level of service. There will come a time when you need to show how well your team is delivering. Some other department head might complain that you are not being very responsive. This may or may not be true. You can find out and produce a report straight out of Jira Service Desk that shows your average time to respond and the number of requests that did not meet the SLA. The point is, with reporting, you can know exactly how your team is doing, and you can respond to managers who want to complain or just want to know how well you are performing.

We use two reports.

Workload: This is a simple report that lists each member of the marketing team and how many requests they have in progress. If I see one person with a lot of requests in progress, I get worried that team member is overloaded. It is an opportunity to step up and help the team.

Time to first response: Our time to first response report shows two things: the average time to first response and a trend line showing whether the time to first response is trending up (bad) or trending down (good).

Jira Service Desk comes with several reports configured right out-of-the-box to make it easy on you to start monitoring your team's performance. But you can customize those reports quite easily to suit your needs.

Integration with Confluence for self-service

This is embarrassing for me to write. My favorite Jira Service Desk function is the integration of Confluence pages right into a service desk request form. And we don't use it. I cannot, therefore, show you how we use it. I will say this, we don't use it for two reasons:

We have not created a knowledge base of how-to articles to show. We have a pretty good process library and our brand assets page is used a lot, and we could have these pages show up on our request form for these topics.

The volume of requests we get has not been so high that the pain of responding to requests has been a problem enough to do something about. So, I'll be honest, we have not needed to help employees serve themselves.

Integrating Confluence and Jira Service Desk will work well for larger marketing teams that have large and widely dispersed stakeholders to service, which includes field and highly decentralized marketing teams.

How Jira Service Desk works with scrum

Remember when I said Jira Service Desk does not directly work for scrum? This is true with one caveat. Sometimes, requests from employees become projects than need to be planned for. When that happens, you take the request and then start planning tasks in your other Jira Software projects and get them into your sprint planning process.

Let's go back to the example I mentioned at the beginning of this chapter. Your HR team wants marketing support for a career expo. Here's how that unplanned work could turn into planned work.

In response to the HR request in Jira Service Desk, you might say, "We are happy to help. We have most of what you need, but we will need to create new brochures and order some more branded notebooks. We are going to close this request and create a set of issues to track all of this."

Then, you would meet with the HR manager and work out the details of the project and track all of that in your sprint planning process until you deliver what they requested. You close out the issue in Jira Service Desk to indicate you have received their request and resolved it by committing to giving HR what it requested. Also, you don't leave one request open in Jira Service Desk with HR for 6 weeks while you do all the work. This type of work is why you use scrum.

8. How We Work in the Real World

"Have a bias towards action — let's see something happen now. You can break that big plan into small steps and take the first step right away."

~ Indira Gandhi

We have spent the bulk of Part Two, describing how we set up Jira Software, Confluence, and Jira Service Desk to run scrum. I wrote conceptually about our configuration rather than show screenshots and get too detailed about how certain features work. I believe understanding concepts and what is possible in software is far more significant and effective than learning how specific features work. I hope now you think so too.

Now it is time to solidify your understanding of agile marketing. In this chapter, I will describe, in as much detail as possible, how we use scrum. I intend to be open and candid about how we work. After reading this chapter, you will be able to visualize how your team would implement scrum. With that said, I believe this is the most important chapter in the book not because I describe how perfectly we implement scrum. If anything, we run it imperfectly. This chapter is valuable because you will learn from the real day-to-day processes of scrum and we actually do it.

Let's dive in with a peek into our sprint planning process.

Sprint planning

We run two-week sprints, so we meet every other Wednesday from 10 am to 12 pm Pacific time. There are seven members of our marketing team. Four of us are in our Palo Alto headquarters, three of us are in our Santiago office, and one of us works remotely.

Our meetings are done by video. We use BlueJeans, and instead of recording the meetings we broadcast them live on Workplace by Facebook in our open marketing group. We work out loud. Anyone in the company can watch our meetings and even comment. We can also go back to review old meetings since the live broadcasts are automatically saved on Workplace by Facebook. Our sprint planning meetings begin with a light, 10 – 15-minute retrospective.

We ask three questions:

1. What went well?
2. What did not go well?
3. What could we do to improve the effectiveness of our sprints?

We combine both the retrospective meeting and the sprint planning in one. I am not sure if this is the best approach. We should spend more time on the retrospective so we learn better and make improvements. We have a retrospective template in Confluence, and we use that template for taking notes. The template automatically creates a place on the page to add the list of meeting attendees and an area to make notes on each of the three questions. After we do the retrospective meeting, we save the page and move on to sprint planning.

We switch from Confluence to now sharing the backlog page from Jira Software. The backlog is a list of all of the tasks we have not yet planned. The list is long. We have hundreds of issues on our backlog. Way too many to manage, and way too many to scroll through during a two-hour meeting. Make no mistake, in a sprint planning meeting you are supposed to go through most of the issues in the backlog and make decisions on what you will work on and finish in the next two weeks. Thank goodness for quick filters. To remind you, we have three kinds of quick filters.

1. One for each line of business
2. One for each member of the team
3. One for projects we think should stand on their own

We often start a sprint planning meeting with one line of business. We just pick one to start with. We click on the quick filter for that line of business and Jira filters the backlog and only shows issues for that line of business. Then, we ask, "What are the most important things we should be getting done in the next two weeks for this line of business?"

The fun begins.

The head of marketing helps prioritize, sharing with the team, high-level priorities learned from the executive team. This gives us a place to start. Sometimes what we have been working on changes direction due to what the executive team works on. Other times, we know what the priorities are and just start talking about those.

Someone chimes in, "Well, we have that Jira Governance Workshop next month. So, in the next two weeks, we need to finish up the presentation slides, add a call to action in the next newsletter promoting the event, and send a second invite to existing customers who are local."

I may ask a few questions:

- Can you get all of that done in the next two weeks?
- What do you need to make that happen?
- Do you have issues already here in the backlog?

I ask whether someone can get all of that done in the next two weeks to remind the team that each individual owns what they add to the sprint. Not me or anyone else. Only a team member can decide what they commit to in a sprint. I cannot assign a task to someone unless they agree they can actually do it. Ownership matters. This is one of the best ways to ensure all or most of what gets done in a sprint actually happens. Because the individual owned the decision to add it to the sprint.

Regarding the second question about whether an issue already exists in Jira, the marketing manager responds, "I have issues in the backlog for the presentation slides and the call to action, but not for the second email. I will create that one now."

While the marketing manager creates that issue in Jira, I will find the two other issues from the list and drag those up to the top of the screen to add both to the sprint. That is quite literally what I do, and what makes Jira so easy to use during a sprint planning session. You find an issue from the backlog. Then drag it up the screen and into the sprint.

We could spend 10 – 30 minutes on one line of business having these discussions. "What else should we work on and get done in the next two weeks?" We discuss what we can do and commit to it by dragging the issue from the backlog up into the sprint.

Sprint planning is not about planning new work for each two-week cycle. Most of the time, we are planning tasks for projects that are currently underway. For example, we may have planned a webinar four weeks ago and during this meeting, we are planning to make more progress on the webinar. When a task, like a webinar, will take longer than one sprint to complete, we use an epic issue type.

Epics are a big deal in scrum, so it is worth spending a considerable amount of time explain how we use them.

How we use epics

The concept of an epic issue type in Jira Software can be confusing. But once you see how an epic is used in the real world, it will clear things up. We have learned what an epic is earlier in the book. And just to reiterate, we will distinguish an epic from other issue types by remembering that a normal issue type is a task that is started and completed in a single sprint. An epic is a task that is completed over multiple sprints.

The best way to understand an epic is to see it in action. This is an example of how we use the epic issue type to plan a webinar. A webinar is a perfect type of work to demonstrate the use of an epic because a webinar is a task that is done across multiple weeks. Think about it. If you look at each individual task you need to perform to run a webinar, the list can become quite long and not all of those tasks are going to occur in a single sprint.

So, to plan a webinar, we create an epic issue type called "Webinar: Name/Topic of Webinar." Once we have created that epic, we open it in Jira and then click on the "plus" sign to add issues to the epic. We start adding each task we will need to complete to run this webinar. That list of tasks will look something like this:

Pick and date
Select topic
Book guest speaker
Write webinar description

Publish landing/registration page
Write email invitations
Schedule/send email invites
Write blog in related topic with call to action to webinar
Write social media posts
Schedule social media posts
Create slide content
Review slide content
Do a run-through with guest speaker
Run the webinar
Upload recording to landing page
Send recording to registrants
Post webinar slides on SlideShare
Write blog recap of webinar

I am sure you can think of more or better tasks, but this list is an example of the types of tasks we need to run a webinar. Notice, also, that these issues will occur over time. Booking the guest speaker will happen very early in the process, whereas writing a recap blog of the webinar will occur near the end of the webinar project, possibly six weeks after the project started.

That list above is now in your backlog. During the sprint planning meeting, we will have our backlog up on the screen and shared on the BlueJeans meeting. With the backlog up, we click on view epics, scroll down the list of epics, and click on the "Webinar: Name/Topic." When we click on that epic, our backlog will show only the issues we created above that are related to the epic.

As we decide which of the webinar tasks to do in this sprint, we simply drag each issue from the backlog, up into the sprint. When we are done, we have the following webinar tasks in the sprint:

Sprint 1

Pick and date
Select topic
Book guest speaker
Write webinar description

That does not seem like a very long list, but it is what we decided as a team we can complete during this sprint, among the other work we have planned. After that sprint is over, we repeat the process described above and drag the following webinar issues into the next sprint. Like this.

Sprint 2

Publish landing/registration page
Write email invitations
Schedule/send email invites
Write blog in related topic with call to action to webinar

We repeat the process again for the third sprint and drag these issues up into the third sprint.

Sprint 3

Write social media posts
Schedule social media posts
Create slide content
Review slide content
Do a run through with guest speaker

The final tasks for our webinar epic will be completed in the fourth sprint, so during sprint planning, we bring up the backlog again, click on the webinar epic, and then drag the final issues into the fourth sprint. Shown below:

Sprint 4

Run webinar
Upload recording to landing page
Send recording to registrants
Post webinar slides on SlideShare
Write blog recap of webinar

And that is how we use an epic issue type to plan a major task over multiple sprints.

On naming sprints

Notice above, I listed each sprint as sprint 1, sprint 2, sprint 3, and sprint 4. Those names are pretty boring, and Jira Software lets you give a name to each sprint. We name our sprints and we have fun doing it.

We have a Confluence page in our marketing space, called "Sprint Names." On that page, we listed a bunch of sprint names using the checklist feature in Confluence. This is the actual list as of this writing.

Taming of the Sprint
Comedy of Sprints
Love's Labor's Sprint
Merchant of Sprint
Merry Wives of Sprint
Montezuma's Revenge
Rodrigo's Revenge

Much Ado About Sprint
Midsummer's Night Sprint
Two Sprints of Verona
Atlas Sprinted
The Red Badge of Sprint
Master SPRINTer
Cookies & Sprint
Merry Sprint
New Year's Sprint
50 Shades of Sprint

Yes, someone on our team likes Shakespeare. What of it? Anyone on the team can add names to the list. And once we have used a name, we click on a checkbox next to the name to indicate it has been used.

I share this only to show you what is possible in Jira Software, and to show a fun way to name your sprints. You likely already have ideas spinning around in your head right now about how to name your sprints.

C'mon have some fun.

Daily stand up

Once we have planned the sprint, we meet every morning in the daily stand up. We have a meeting on the calendar at 9 am Pacific time every day of the week, except on the Wednesdays when we do our retrospective and sprint planning. Everyone on the team is expected to attend the meeting, but we understand when someone cannot. When someone cannot attend a stand up, they post a message on Workplace answering the three daily stand up questions.

The meetings are brief. Everyone joins the BlueJeans video meeting and for those in offices together, they gather in a conference room. When we first started with scum, our stand up quickly became an update meeting on anything we were working on, including talking about meetings we had scheduled that day. The purpose of the daily stand up is to advance the sprint, not give everyone a status update and show everyone your schedule.

To correct this aimlessness, we focused on these three questions:

1. What did you do to advance the sprint yesterday?
2. What will you do the advance the sprint today?
3. What is getting in your way?

Let's go back to our webinar example to demonstrate how our daily stand ups go. If the webinar is my project, I will say at my turn, "Yesterday, to advance the sprint, I picked the date and selected the topic for the webinar and spoke with two potential guest speakers who gave me a verbal yes."

Then I will say, "Today, to advance the sprint, I plan to get confirmation from one of the guest speakers that they can do the webinar on that date. I'll book it on the calendar when I do."

"I have no blockers (nothing is getting in my way)."

That's it. I may have other work on my list. But if I am sticking to the stand up process, I only discuss the items in the sprint that I have completed yesterday or are going to finish today. And discuss what is preventing me from getting those issues done.

Sometimes we stray

Our daily stand ups are generally that efficient, but not always. There are times when we give updates to the team that are not specifically related to advancing the sprint. Sometimes an update might sound like this:

"Today, I have the weekly Workplace by Facebook offerings meeting and I need to talk to Paula about the Facebook ad results that we tested." There might be no issue in the sprint specifically. This is a bad update. This team member should only discuss progress on planned work. Sometimes we are strict about it and sometimes we are not.

When we are strict, I'll say, "What issue does that relate to?" or, "Is there an issue for that?" or, "What issue did you complete yesterday on that?"

The team member will say, "I don't have an issue for that. OK, got it. The two issues I am working on today are..." That is how we get back on track. You really do have to be focused. This is the job of the scrum master. To make sure scrum is followed and that the sprint is being advanced each day.

Backlog grooming

It all started about one year into our use of scrum. I had this earth-shattering idea to do backlog grooming. Actually, backlog grooming is not earth-shattering. Every scrum team that does scrum properly does backlog grooming. We had not.

When I had this idea, it was a day I was going through our backlog right before a sprint planning meeting. There were 1,176 issues in the backlog. Obviously, we are heavy Jira users. That is way too many issues to stay on top of, and it can slow down a sprint planning meeting going through all those issues. Since we had not been very disciplined about prioritizing our backlog, issues that we should plan for in the next sprint, could very well be way down that list.

So, my brilliant idea was more like a wake-up call. "We better start grooming this backlog before it gets out of control." At the beginning of that sprint meeting I told the team, "I'd like to schedule meetings in the next week or two to go through our backlog, get rid of old issues we will never get to, prioritize the issues we have, and even add new items that we have not documented yet. We gotta clear this backlog out. How about we do a two-hour meeting next Friday?"

To my surprise, everyone agreed.

During that meeting, we went through all of those issues and cut our backlog by about a third. This is how we did it. Since there were so many issues, we did not go through the raw list of issues. We started by clicking on each epic in our backlog.

On the backlog screen in Jira, you can show all epics on the left side. If you click on the first epic, all of the issues associated with that epic show up on the backlog in the middle of the screen. We looked at the epic itself and asked, "Will we still work on this epic?" If the answer is no, then we can close the epic and all issues in that epic. That simple act could close out a dozen issues in one shot. If we still need to work on that epic, we reviewed all the issues for that epic and decided as a team what issues should remain, what issues should be removed (or changed) and what issues we needed to add.

When we were done with that epic, we clicked on the next epic on the list and did the same thing. We went through all of our epics and cleaned them up. It was quite satisfying. After we finished with the epics, we started going through the issues not associated with epics. We did not do this in any magical way. We simply clicked on each quick filter at the top of the backlog (if you recall, we have quick filters for lines of business, each member of the team, and for unassigned issues) and went through the individual issues and reviewed as a team whether to keep or close them. The process was tedious and exhilarating and satisfying. We closed numerous issues that were done, but just never got closed. We closed numerous issues that we knew we would never get to. Our priorities had changed and the need to deliver those items were no longer needed.

We agreed, as a team, that we would continue with these extended backlog grooming meetings and do them quarterly. After that first backlog grooming session, I realized that I dramatically underappreciated backlog grooming.

If you read between the lines in scrum, you realize that you really have to fall in love with your backlog. At least once before each sprint, you should spend time with your backlog doing each of the following:

- Grooming
- Prioritizing
- Estimating
- Refining
- Repeat

Some scrum teams do mini backlog grooming meetings for 30 minutes before each sprint planning meeting. Perhaps the day before sprint planning.

Fall in love with your backlog.

We even do a little reporting

My favorite report in Jira is the created versus resolved report. It is a simple trend line report that shows a comparison between the number of issues created in a project and the number of issues completed during the past 30 days.

It is a general report of activity for the team. When you are creating more issues than you resolve, and this persists over time, it is a clue that your team is not completing what they started. It is a good chart to view at each retrospective meeting as a team and just talk briefly about how the activity is going based on the chart.

We have also, on these dashboards, a report on the average age of issues. This should show the average number of days an issue remains opened. If the line trends higher, it is a possible bad sign. The team is adding issues to the backlog and not working on them/completing them.

Perfection was never the goal

That was a peek at some of how are team runs scrum. If you have paid attention throughout this book, you may have read this chapter and asked yourself, "He left out a lot of stuff. What about estimating? What about the sprint review?" These are good questions. I will admit that we did not execute scrum perfectly when we started. This was intentional. Our bias was to start, to learn, and to improve. We ignored some scrum functions, made some mistakes in our initial Jira Software configuration, and were sometimes undisciplined.

To address the elephant in the room, I explain in Part Three the mistakes we made and what we plan to put in place to improve how we run scrum. I hope you learn from our mistakes. More importantly, I hope you come away from Part Three with the belief that you don't have to implement agile marketing perfectly either. You don't have to be a scrum master. You just need the courage to start. Starting is often the hardest part. I hope to make starting a little easier.

Part Three
[Trusting the Process]

9. The Mistakes We Made

"Anyone who has never made a mistake has never tried anything new."

~ Albert Einstein

A common aphorism is to say, "learn from my mistakes so you don't make them yourself." But that is not what this chapter is about. I do want you to learn from our mistakes so as not to repeat them. You might discover something we considered a mistake would work perfectly for your team. I also want to help you understand that it is OK to make your own mistakes, and that it is OK to get started using scrum and not do everything perfectly right from the start. It is more important to get started than it is to roll out scrum perfectly. You need to start the "doing," make your own mistakes, and discover better ways of working.

One of the best things about doing agile in Jira Software is you can continuously make changes to Jira. At some point, you need to leave Jira alone and just work for a consistent period of time with the configuration you created. You will gain experience working in Jira Software and running scrum; you will discover mistakes and new ways you could adjust to improve how you work. But understand that you can start with minimum configurations, get started, and gain experience as a team running scrum. Experience matters. Scrum will become a habit when you do.

Developing new habits takes time

Just this week (as I write this) the calendar invite for our daily stand ups expired. I guess I had it set to recur for one year. Anyway, there was no calendar invite for our stand up on a Tuesday. Our stand ups are scheduled for 9:00 am every weekday except on days when we do sprint planning. On this particular Tuesday morning at 8:45 am, our chat room in Workplace by Facebook blew up with team members asking, "Are we having stand up today?" Gifs, memes, and statements of despair were filling up the stream. There was no way our team was going to let us skip our stand up just because the calendar invite expired.

At 8:52, we sent out a new calendar invite to recur forever, spun up a new Bluejeans link and started stand up (almost) on-time.

This is what will happen when you start running scrum. People will want to attend meetings because they are so useful. They have a purpose. And a pre-defined agenda. Even if you don't practice them perfectly at the beginning. Developing habits like this will take time, but they can happen.

Let's get on with our first mistake.

Working in one project with multiple issue types

In an attempt to make things simple at the beginning of our scrum journey, we decided to create one project in Jira called

"Marketing" (MKT). We then created issue types for each type of work we do. Here is an example of the issue types we had.

- Podcast
- Webinar
- Event
- Web optimization
- Graphics request
- Schwag request
- Content
- Advertising

One of the main reasons we used issue types instead of projects to organize our work was too make reporting on work easier. We could use the reporting tools in Jira to report on the activity for each issue type. Think about that for a minute. One of our primary reasons we set up Jira in this way was to make reporting easier. Who does that? We thought we were smart thinking ahead like that. We knew we would want to run performance reports in Jira to measure our work, so we took a design step up front to make reporting easier. That sounds forward thinking right? Maybe it was.

Most teams don't consider reporting on their work when they start using a work tool. They just think about the work, and then work out how to run reports on performance later. By then, reporting is difficult and you don't have the data or the reporting tools set up properly to do it. So, you export a lot, manually add things to a spreadsheet and use pivot tables and sorting and macros to figure things out. It's awful. No wonder most teams ignore reporting and just move on to the next project. But we were smart. Except that we weren't.

This decision to consider reporting up front and work in one project with all issue types, was letting the tail wag the dog. It made the daily act of working frustrating and tedious. In one small example, let's consider the simple task of creating a new issue in a project. Because we have all of our issue types in one project, every time someone creates a new issue, they have to scroll down through the list of all issue types to pick the one they want.

This seems insignificant until you realize one person does most of their work in only a few issue types. Our creative director spends most of his time working on issues for graphics, for example. If the graphics issue is on the bottom of the list, then every time he creates a new graphics issue, he has to scroll down to the bottom of the list to select it. Apply that to every member of the team, multiple times per day, over several weeks and it starts to get annoying.

What issue type should I choose?

The more specialized our issue types and the more issue types we had, the more choices we had. We spent a lot of time asking ourselves, "What issue type should I choose?" Let's say we want to run a webinar next month. It seems like an easy decision. We created a webinar issue type. Well, I could argue a webinar is an event, so why not use the event issue type? It was these little, day-to-day decisions that prompted us to make some changes.

Jira is designed so you can create projects, which are areas in which certain types of work are sectioned off from the rest, making it easier to focus on that work. We eventually redesigned this and created a project for each major work type we have.

Setting up one project with all issues types in it was a mistake.

Over customized and thought everything was special

Have you ever used software that had so any fields on the page, and you don't even use 90% of those fields? Have you ever used

Salesforce? That is how we designed our issue types at the beginning. When we planned the webinar issue type, we created a custom field called "Webinar Date" to indicate when the webinar would be delivered. Sounds smart, right? Wrong. We never used it. Why not? Jira comes with a field called "Due Date," we just used that. There is a reason to have a due date and a webinar date. The webinar is not actually done when we deliver the webinar. There are post-webinar tasks. We just never used the webinar date field, so why have it?

This was not the only example. We created several custom fields in the webinar issue type.

- Guest speaker
- Webinar type
- Line of business
- Target audience
- Target product
- Call to action
- Webinar goal

There is nothing wrong with any of these custom fields. In fact, every time we run a webinar, we should know all of these. In the real world, we either don't know the answer to one of these yet, or we just typed it into the main description field on the issue. Therefore, none of these fields ever got used after the first webinar or two. When we created a webinar issue type, the description field looked like this, "Let's do a webinar in February on Jira Governance and try to get one of our customers as a guest speaker. We will cover the following topics: this, that, and the other thing."

Do we really need a custom field for each phrase in that description? I can read that and know what work needs to be done. And that is the most important part.

Creating too many custom fields was a mistake

Customized workflows: In progress means different things to different people

If you consider the long list of issue types we created, you can imagine each of those issue types have a different workflow. We did. So, we created a custom workflow for each of those issue types. We created workflow steps called setup, publish, requested, in progress, working, in review, review, done, finished, completed, etc. How many ways do we have to say done or in progress or in review?

Isn't work either in some form of not started, in progress, in review, and finished? As I write this (and probably as you read this), it seems silly that we would create four ways to say done: done, completed, finished, published. But we did. It is a lot easier to go down that road than you think.

There certainly are examples when you need a unique workflow. Some of you, who need to get legal approval before you publish a blog, should probably have a workflow step called "In Legal." But as our friend, Vilfredo Pareto once advised us, most of your work types run through the same workflow.

The biggest problem these custom workflows caused was in monitoring our work. Let's say you want to search for all event issues that are in progress. The purpose of this search is to find out what events are in progress, so you can help get them done or find out why they are not done yet. Jira has a very powerful tool for search. Using filters, I can select the issue type "events" then select the workflow stage, "In progress." This will show a list of all events tasks that are in progress. I can scroll up and down this list and close the ones that are actually finished (sometimes we forget to close issues). I can also see that someone on the team is working on an issue and ask in the comments, "Is this almost done? Need anything from me?"

Filters in Jira are magical.

Except when there are 12 workflow stages using some euphemism for in progress. When I scroll through the status filter looking for the in progress status, which one do I pick? I forget the name we used for the in progress workflow step for the events issue type. Should I then just pick all of them? The one I think it is? Maybe I should go to the admin console, look up the event workflow and then go back to my filter and set it. I want to pull my hair out just thinking about it.

Creating too many custom workflows was a mistake.

Hastened sprint planning meetings

The appropriate length of a sprint planning meeting was looking right at me in Brinker's book, *Hacking Marketing: Agile Practices to Make Marketing Smarter, Faster, and More Innovative.* He suggests sprint planning meetings should be two hours for each week of a sprint. We run two-week sprints, so our sprint planning meetings should be four hours. Despite Brinker's solid advice, we started off with two-hour planning meetings. And they felt too long.

I wanted to do all of the planning in that meeting and get all of the issues created and into the sprint, while we're all sitting in the meeting. I made a mistake assuming that there was a lot of wasted time watching each other create issues and add them to the sprint. Based on this assumption, we decided to make the meeting shorter. The meeting became talking about the issues to add to the sprint, and then end the meeting to let everyone leave to go create their issues and get them into the sprint later in the day. I would start the sprint at the end of the day.

Guess what. I got our time back to work on things. But almost never did everyone create all their issues and get them into the sprint before I started it. The consequence was that we spent way too much time on unplanned and reactionary work. We did not fully commit to the sprint because we hadn't planned it properly as a team. We went back to the longer meetings. We stayed in those meetings until all the issues were created and the sprint was started. With few exceptions.

Not committing to a proper sprint planning meeting was a mistake.

Undisciplined stand ups

At first, the team resisted the daily stand up. Daily? Isn't that too many meetings? "The point," I said, "was that these meetings will help us hold each other accountable and move the sprint along. And they will only be 15 minutes. Max." So everyone agreed.

Side note: The meeting is called a stand up because if you stand up during the meeting, it makes everyone want to end the meeting quickly. No one wants to stand for a long meeting. So, if your team is all in one office, then stand up when you have the meeting. Go find a nice common area to hold your stand ups and actually stand. We have a remote team, so we don't stand up. Maybe we should, even on a video call.

The mistake we made in our stand ups was not being disciplined about moving the sprint forward. Our stand up became status updates about anything we were working on, including unplanned work (stuff not in the sprint) and tasks that didn't even have an issue in Jira.

At the beginning, we asked ourselves these questions:

1. What did you work on yesterday?
2. What are you working on today?
3. What is getting in your way?

In the book, *Hacking Marketing*, Scott Brinker described similar questions to use during the stand up:

1. What did I do yesterday?
2. What will I do today?
3. Are there any impediments that may prevent me, or the team, from accomplishing our goals for the sprint?

For some reason, our team used these questions to talk about anything we wanted. Imagine this update from me, "Yeah you know, I am working on setting up a meeting with Janet. She told me she could meet tomorrow, so we're working on that to talk about the ad campaign we are running to look into the numbers to see if the results are positive." As an un-certified scrum master, I did not pick up on this meandering as quickly as you'd think.

It took a few weeks to get disciplined. Even though we knew to focus on the three questions, we didn't. Things started to pick up when we changed how we asked the three questions:

1. What did you accomplish yesterday to advance the sprint?
2. What will you accomplish today to advance the sprint?
3. What is getting in your way?

Everyone, once in a while, would veer off, and I asked the team, "What is the issue for that? Oh, there isn't one. I'll create it." Jeff Sutherland, in his book, *Scrum: The Art of Doing Twice the Work in Half the Time*, suggests these three questions:

1. What did you do yesterday to help the team finish the sprint?
2. What will you do today to help the team finish the sprint?
3. What obstacles are getting in the team's way?

Sutherland co-created scrum, so we might want to listen. Running undisciplined daily stand ups was a mistake.

Setting up our own Jira instance

When we started running scrum, we set up our own Jira Software instance and only members of the marketing team have access. That is also why we set up Jira Service Desk, to provide a means for the rest of the company to interact with marketing and request services.

We didn't need to buy our own Jira Software instance. We have a Jira instance at ServiceRocket that all employees have access to. We could have set up our projects in that Jira, and not paid extra for our own Jira.

We set up our own Jira instance because we wanted more control over our configuration, and we wanted to be more responsive in making changes. It is a lot easier to change our own Jira because changes only affect our small team. To make changes to any software that impacts all employees, they need to go through a proper change process. Since we are such a small marketing team, we decided to set up our own and have more control.

Setting up our own Jira instance may have been a mistake. I'd like to walk you through the reasons for buying our own Jira, even though it might not have been a mistake, because I think it will help you decide whether you should set up your own Jira or use one that your organization already uses (assuming it does). There are two main reasons it might have been a mistake.

Working in a silo: With our own Jira instance, only members of the marketing team have access to it. That seems reasonable for most work. However, the more we collaborate with stakeholders, the more isolated our work feels. When we do a go-to-market plan for a new product launch, we work on our plan, isolated from the product team, who does not have access to our Jira. Product launches require a team effort. If the product team also had access to our projects, we could work together in real time. This example applies to work we do with any team at ServiceRocket. If we worked in our company-wide Jira, we would always have the ability to pull other teams into our projects or collaborate in theirs.

Taking on an extra expense: Why would we spend money on our own Jira instance when ServiceRocket already has a Jira that all employees have access to, including the marketing team. Our marketing team spends about $1,200 per year on our own Jira. It is not a lot of money, but it is an additional amount of money. We wanted to make the investment because we wanted a little control over managing our instance. Maybe we don't need control or the extra cost for the benefit of working in a silo.

[I think] Buying our own Jira instance was a mistake.

To silo or not to silo

When you evaluate whether to use Jira to manage your projects, you will need to decide who should have access. If your company already uses Jira, consider strongly setting up your agile marketing processes in that Jira. The more open and connected you are with the rest of your organization the better.

On the other hand, if getting your agile marketing practices set up on that Jira will take longer than you want, get your own. Jira is inexpensive, and you can get started more quickly. Starting matters. Gaining experience matters. Learning matters. Delivering highly predictable and effective marketing campaigns that help grow your company matters. If your company does not use Jira, obviously, you should get your own.

Learn from your mistakes

The best thing about a mistake is the opportunity it creates to make an improvement. In the next chapter, we will discuss some of the improvements we have planned in our agile marketing practices.

10. Where We Are Headed

"Enjoy the journey and try to get better every day. And don't lose the passion and the love for what you do."

~ Nadia Comaneci

I think it is clear by now that our agile marketing implementation was not perfect. There were many tradeoffs, decisions without full knowledge, and deliberate decisions made not to implement certain functions of agile marketing. I have argued throughout this book that "starting now" is better than getting caught up in the details that could slow us down. The sooner we start, the sooner we gain experience, gain skill, gain knowledge, and gain the ability to improve.

In this chapter, I describe four improvements we plan to make. These are:

1. Estimating our work
2. Write stories, not tasks
3. Start doing sprint reviews
4. Fall way more in love with our backlog

Let's get started.

Estimating our work

I think the unsung hero of scrum is estimating, but I have been afraid to implement it. It seems like extra tedious work in a sprint planning meeting, and I have not wanted to impose that in our already lengthy meetings. This is a mistake, as you will soon discover.

I also assume most people on the team are smart enough to know which and how many tasks they can accomplish during a sprint. The data tells another story. We are not good at determining how much work we can accomplish during a sprint. We continuously overestimate. I know this because Jira tells me. Each time you close out a sprint, Jira tells you how many tasks the team completed and how many did not get completed.

Our problem is that during sprint planning, we go through our backlog and say, "Well, it has to get done so... I guess I'll just put it in the sprint." This is a major mistake. If that task must get done, it means other tasks should not be added to the sprint. When you don't know how much work you can get done, you cannot plan. And you cannot plan until you know how much work you can get done. The only way to know how much work you can get done is to start estimating your work for each sprint, measure it after each sprint. After a few sprints, you will know how much work you can get done.

In the book, *Scrum: The Art of Doing Twice the Work in Half the Time*, Jeff Sutherland tells an excellent story about how estimating can work to improve how teams know exactly how much work they can handle and how good estimating makes it very easy to adapt and react to changing priorities during a sprint.

The short version of the story is that a team has (let's say) 100 points of work planned for the current sprint. Something comes along with a new priority. It is urgent. It has to get done. The CEO said so. Your attempts to say, "Our sprint is locked down. we'll put it in our backlog and plan for it in the next sprint," fail.

What to do? We are already loaded and our plates are full. The unsustainable solution is to just add this new work to your sprint and work longer hours. This is fine. Occasionally. But we cannot allow ourselves to be caught in the habit. So, the team sits down to estimate the work. Using the story point method, the team figures this new work will take 50 story points.

What scrum allows you to do is say, "OK, we need to remove 50-points worth of work we have already planned so we can add this new 50-points worth of work." We cannot just add. We have to replace. And we have to make this decision as a team. The team members need to figure this out and decide how.

That story paints a clear picture of what life could be like if an agile marketing team uses story points.

Story points: How estimating works

We estimate every day. Every time we answer the question, "Can you get that done by Friday?" We estimate in our heads. Sometimes we are right. Sometimes we are wrong, and we stay late the night before to finish up. Estimating this way is a crapshoot. There is no method. It's just a guess.

Estimating with story points is a method for estimating. A method from which we can learn and, over time, get really good at estimating. When you get good at estimating, work becomes very predictable. You will get very good at knowing how much work you can get done in a sprint and have the confidence to share that with your key stakeholders. So, I've read. Like I said, we did not estimate during the early parts of our scrum journey.

One problem with estimating: The one problem with estimating is doing it during sprint planning. It was for us, anyway.

THE ART OF AGILE MARKETING

Running a sprint planning meeting, adding issues to Jira and then to the sprint, while everyone else on the team watches you AND then estimating with points? That seemed like too many things to do. But that limiting belief changed for me when I learned that part of good backlog grooming includes estimating.

This was an "aha" moment for me. I used to think estimating was part of sprint planning. It should not be. Estimating should be part of backlog grooming. Estimating should be done before sprint planning.

Here's why.

If sprint planning is the process of planning what work will get done during the sprint, you have to know how much work you can get done in the sprint. To know how much work you can get done in a sprint, you have to know how many story points you can get done in a sprint. For example, if you know you can handle 25 story points during a sprint and each (or most) of your issues already have story points on them, you know when to stop adding to the sprint...when you reach 25. It is a built-in regulator.

Our team constantly over plans sprints. We add too many issues and rarely complete all the work we planned. Because we don't estimate. We plan to change that. I want our work to be more predictable. So do our stakeholders.

To learn more about how estimating works, I'd read Jeff Sutherland's book, *Scrum: The Art of Doing Twice the Work in Half the Time*. I believe he describes how to do it best.

Write stories, not tasks

Speaking of stories. The best and most focused scrum teams don't document, plan, and execute tasks. They write "user stories." For us in marketing, we should think in terms of customer stories. A story is a more customer-focused way of writing a task.

Brinker offers a template for how to write a customer story that I find quite helpful:

As a BUYER's ROLE, I would like CONTENT OR EXPERIENCE so that BENEFIT/REASON WHY.

Brinker translates that into a story with this example:

As a mid-funnel prospect, I would like a pricing guide and interactive pricing calculator so that we can determine whether your solution will fit in our budget.

Brinker goes on to say, "Well written stories push strategic thinking deeper into the front lines of marketing." I say it makes us much more customer-focused because a story turns a task into something that reflects what a customer wants.

Taking Brinker's example above, if we write a task, "Create an interactive pricing guide," we make an assumption about the solution. Once we deliver that solution (the guide), we are done. The guide might even miss the mark. If we write a story, as Brinker suggests, you know that what the customer wants is a tool to help them discover whether your solution is priced within their budget. This story is helpful and inspires you to create a solution to help that customer with their needs.

Stories are a very different way of looking at the world, and the more we write our tasks as stories, the better marketing we will deliver. This is especially true if we can align these stories with the buyer journey.

Brinker says it well: "And if we can write these stories in the context of the buyer journey, we will master the art of tailoring our marketing to buyer needs at each stage of the journey."

Let's use the buyer journey model from HubSpot to show how this might work:

Awareness stage: I am discovering this problem.

Instead of writing a task like this:

> Write a blog post about how to motivate a team.

Write a story like this:

> A project manager is having a hard time getting team members to update their tasks but doesn't know why.

See how the second one puts yourself in the mind of the buyer? So, in that story we can do a lot of things in marketing to help that person, including writing a blog post to help that project manager discover the nature of that problem.

Consideration stage: I am discovering a solution to this problem.

Instead of writing a task like this:

> Write a blog post called 3 ways to remind your team with software automation.

Write a story like this:

> I wish there was a way to automatically remind my team without me having to check up on their everyday.

Decision stage: I am discovering products that help me solve this problem.

Instead of writing a task like this:

> Create a matrix comparing our product to our competitors' products.

Write a story like this:

> There are so many choices, how do I decide on a product. I don't want to make a mistake and be locked into a product that doesn't work for us.

Think about how much better our marketing would be if we wrote stories like this instead of tasks. It will take some practice, but we plan to start writing customer stories.

Start doing sprint reviews

I confess. When I started learning about scrum, I did not make the distinction between the retrospective and the sprint review. So, we really only did retrospectives. A retrospective is about reviewing the process. A sprint review is a meeting to show stakeholders what we delivered at the end of the sprint. This is the entire point of agile marketing: to deliver some specific, usable, valuable, work product, collect feedback from stakeholders, and use that feedback in the next sprint to make improvements.

Here is an example. If we are writing a white paper, we may have planned to write the creative brief during this sprint. In the sprint review meeting, we would show that creative brief to the product manager and get their feedback. That is how we gain early feedback from the "customer" and adjust if necessary. The feedback we get largely determines what we plan in the next sprint, which could be re-writing the brief or start writing the white paper.

We plan to start doing sprint review meetings and publish them to the entire company. In fact, that would be very easy. We could schedule it using Bluejeans video conference and broadcast it live to Workplace by Facebook platform, so all employees could watch, comment, ask questions, etc. Plus, the video will automatically be saved in Workplace for anyone to watch later.

Fall way more in love with our backlog

When we started, we did not groom our backlog. The backlog just grew and became an overwhelming list of thousands of tasks and ideas. When we finally did our first backlog grooming meeting, the team was instantly relieved. We felt liberated. After that first grooming meeting, we thought scheduling them quarterly was enough. But here's the thing. Quarterly is not nearly enough. Backlog grooming should occur at least as often as a sprint cycle. And backlog grooming is not just about closing old issues. It should include prioritizing issues in the backlog and estimating issues in the backlog. Backlog grooming that includes prioritizing and estimating is precisely why it should be done as often as you run sprints. Let's talk about prioritizing and estimating in backlog grooming.

Prioritizing

The process of prioritizing the backlog in Jira involves scrolling through the list of issues in the backlog and dragging issues up to the top of the list in the approximate order in which you will work on them next. You want to bring, to the top of your backlog, the issues you know you will add to the next sprint.

What makes scrum "agile" is that you do not necessarily know what you are going to prioritize and decide to work on in a future sprint until you complete a current sprint. If what you are working on is well received, you know you will continue with it. But if something changes, you completed change directions and plan different tasks in the next sprint. On the other hand, in most normal circumstances, you pretty much know what your next sprint will be about. This means you have several issues in your backlog that you will work on in future sprints, assuming everything goes to plan.

The act of prioritizing your backlog is moving these issues to the top of your backlog. This is useful because it helps you look into the future, and it makes sprint planning more efficient. For the issues you prioritized, you can easily commit to adding them to the sprint, because you have already gone through the process of prioritizing them. Backlog grooming is a manifestation of the philosophy, "A little working today, makes work tomorrow much easier."

Estimating

The second part of backlog grooming is estimating. There is a rule in scrum that no issue should be put in a sprint until it is estimated. You can save a lot of time in a sprint planning meeting discussing estimates if you do that during backlog grooming.

As you go through your backlog and prioritize issues, think about what the estimate is and add your estimate to the issue. Then, when it's time for sprint planning, you have already thought about the estimate. If someone disagrees with your estimate, you can discuss it. If no one disagrees, you simply add that issue to the sprint and move on.

We plan to do backlog grooming before each sprint, in short 30-minute sessions.

Why we didn't do these things from the beginning

I want to bring this chapter to a close with a discussion about why we did not start doing these scrum fundamentals right from the beginning. It is an important topic because if scrum is so good, why not do it right in the first place?

The secret to life is action. I find that when a new project is large, it is intimidating, and that overwhelming feeling I get often prevents me from acting. Think about anything we want to do in life: get to our ideal weight, learn a new skill, write a book, implement agile marketing. These are big projects that can take many weeks or months of constant work. Just the thought of beginning any of these projects makes me want to rationalize why I will start my diet on Monday.

Whenever I have been successful at starting something new, I just started with one small action. I worked on one small habit, mastered that, and only then did I take on the next step. I took that approach to our agile marketing implementation. I knew that if we started doing everything in scrum perfectly right from the start, it would not have stuck, we would have had too many reasons (excuses) to fall back into old habits. We made deliberate decisions not to do estimating and to write stories. I admit that we didn't do sprint reviews and frequent backlog grooming because it didn't occur to us. The result was the same, we implemented agile marketing and have been consistent about it ever since.

The main advice I offer in this book is this: Don't do it all at first. Start with one thing. Master it. Make it a habit. Then build on it.

Constantly evolve

There is more to it than just starting with some small parts of agile marketing and building on it later. We also made an assumption that we would be constantly evolving how we use Jira Software. Every couple of months, we modify how we use Jira Software, Confluence, and Jira Service Desk. We add reporting widgets to our dashboard to monitor our work better. We change our quick filters to make our meetings more efficient. We create new templates to make planning webinars easier.

It's not like we will get to a point when we say, "Finally, we have Jira set up right and we have our agile processes down."

With this belief, why would we begin a new process like agile marketing with the intention of "doing it right the first time." Maybe there is no "right."

Instead, we learn, we adjust, we improve.

That is the art of agile marketing.

11. Your Implementation Plan

"Action is the foundational key to all success."

~ Pablo Picasso

"Just do it." ~ Nike

The tricky thing about implementing agile marketing is that you are introducing three new processes to your team. First, is agile marketing the belief system. This is a new way of thinking and will take time and deliberate effort to be successful. The second challenge is implementing an agile methodology like scrum or kanban. Although the steps of scrum and kanban are not difficult to understand, they are difficult to do because building new habits is difficult. Third, introducing new software, like Jira, is a challenge because adopting any new software is a challenge.

So, while you are implementing agile marketing, you also have to choose a methodology, and start using new software. This is the trifecta of change management. While we will not cover change management in this book, I recommend you at least make change management a part of your rollout. This chapter is about the technical and functional implementation.

Implementing agile marketing

This outline will help you create your own implementation plan. Feel free to adjust it as necessary. Here are the seven major steps for an effective agile marketing rollout.

1. Decide you want to run agile marketing
2. Choose agile method
3. Document your requirements
4. Get Jira Software and Confluence
5. Configure Jira and Confluence
6. Educate your team
7. Start using it and stay vigilant

Let's go through each step in this process. If I were to plan this implementation using scrum, I would plan two-week sprints, create an epic for each of the seven steps in this plan, then create individual issues for each epic. Then, I would plan my first sprint. You could do this on a whiteboard, with a simple scrum board, sticky notes, and a sharpie.

Let's get to step one.

Step 1: Decide you want to run agile marketing

I am assuming you have already made the decision to go agile. If you have read this far, and If for some reason you still need convincing, you should read Brinker, Fryrear, and Sutherland. I have referenced these experts numerous times in this book, and their books are excellent.

Step 2: Choose the agile method

Choosing the agile method is more art than science. Yes, there are pros and cons of both kanban and scrum. To help you decide, here is how you could pick kanban:

If you...

Believe all of your marketing work is a continuous flow of work that never seems to stop, and you get caught up in having so many things in progress, feeling overwhelmed, and never knowing the current state of things.

If you want to visualize the flow of your work, so it's easy to see what is in progress.

If you want a method for limiting your work in progress, so you don't overcommit your team.

Here is how you could pick scrum:

If you...

Have a lot of project work with end dates.

Feel like you are never prioritized.

React to things as they come up.

Don't know if your team is improving in its effectiveness.

Like the idea of breaking down you work and giving yourself self-improved deadlines.

If you want to get closer to your stakeholder and include their input earlier on in the process.

These are just some criteria for making the decision. To me, it comes down to two simple ideas. If you believe your team would benefit from time-bound, self-imposed deadlines that allow your team to focus on each deadline with prioritized work, scrum is for you. If you believe the work you do is a continuous flow, use kanban.

Yes, it is more complicated than that. If you want it to be. Otherwise, pick one, start using it, learn from it, and adjust. Choosing an agile marketing methodology is not a final decision.

Step 3: Document your requirements

Based on what you have learned in this book so far, you have what
you need to write a basic set of requirements for how to set up
Jira and Confluence. Write down requirements for the following
topics:

Permissions: Who gets access to what and what permission
level they should have.

Issue types: What issue types will you have and what should
the issue type screen look like? What fields should be on each of
those issue types?

Workflows: What will your workflows look like? When in
doubt, use the standard 4-step workflow:

Open > In Progress > In Review > Done.

Remember, each issue type can have its own workflow. Just
don't get too complicated. Workflows are more similar than they
are different.

When in doubt, write your requirements by following the
outlines of Chapter 5: How We Set Up Scrum in Jira and Chapter 6:
How We Set Up Confluence.

Documenting your requirements is important for two reasons.
First, it will help you think through how you want to work in Jira
and Confluence and how you will set it up. Second, documenting
your requirements will make it easier for someone to help you
configure Jira and Confluence, should you need help.

Step 4: Get Jira Software and Confluence

This is about the purchase decision. If you follow the recommendations
in this book, you will need to buy Jira Software, Confluence, and Jira
Service Desk. If you want to run kanban or scrum, but do not want
to set up a service management process to handle requests, don't

buy Jira Service Desk yet. Focus on Jira Software and Confluence. Start by mastering agile before you add Jira Service Desk. Add Jira Service Desk in year two of your agile journey.

Step 5: Configure Jira and Confluence

Setting up Jira Software and Confluence takes some skill. If your company already uses Jira or Confluence, there will be someone in your company with the skills. See if you can get that person to help you configure Jira and Confluence. If you do not have someone at your company who can help you set these up, you can work with a Atlassian Solutions Partner. Atlassian itself does not provide configuration services. Instead, it has built a thriving network of software consulting companies that have expertise helping Atlassian customers set up and get the most out of their investment in Jira and Confluence.

I, of course, suggest that if you want help, you call ServiceRocket. Not only does ServiceRocket have expertise in Jira and Confluence, but we have expertise in how marketing teams can use it, which is to say, "We get you."

Step 6: Educate your team

Getting your team skilled up to use Jira and Confluence is beyond the scope of this book. But any time you introduce new processes and software to a team, there is a need to learn the new way. Using Jira and Confluence is not that difficult to learn. What makes it challenging is understanding the fundamentals. This does not mean you need formal training. It does mean you need to help your team learn it. If you have a tech savvy team, the effort will be minimal. If your team is new to Jira and Confluence, you will need to invest more energy in helping your team learn it.

The best place to start is at Atlassian University. There you will find a variety of learning options, from self-paced online learning to onsite, custom training options. Before you launch any kind of training program, it is best that you already have your Jira and Confluence instances set up. That way, when your team starts to learn it, no matter what type of learning they do, they can go into your Jira and Confluence and start using it for real.

If you choose any type of live training options, I recommend making sure that training is as hands-on as possible. In fact, those training courses should require your team to work on actual work. It should be as real as possible to be most effective.

Step 7: Start using it and stay vigilant

When your team starts using Jira and Confluence and you start running agile marketing, you will need to be vigilant. Your team will hang on to old habits. They will have every good intention during your first several sprint planning meetings and plan the tasks they believe they will get done. Then, they will spend the next several days working on urgent tasks rather than spend any meaningful time on the tasks they planned in the sprint.

Expect this.

When you see it happen, remember you read this. Remember that you can and did see into the future. You will need to stay on your team and constantly remind them to focus on the work they planned. This is done in the daily stand up meetings. If you notice people in stand up start talking about things not in the sprint, let them talk, then gently ask, "What issue in the sprint does that relate to?"

The new habit of focusing people's attention in these meetings on planned work will take time to develop. Just keep people focused on the issues they planned. If something needs to be discussed that is not related to the planned work in the sprint (and there always will be) recommend taking that discussion after the meeting.

What to do if you lead a large marketing team?

If your marketing team is more than 7-10 people, you will want to break your team up into multiple sprint teams of 4-7 people. That is what Andrea Fryrear recommends in her book, *The Death of Marketing*. I agree. You break these teams up by product, line of business, or marketing function. Just make sure to organize your smaller scrum teams in such a way that they are each delivering to the appropriate stakeholders. There could be a scrum team for each of the following:

- Product launches
- Paid media campaigns
- Events
- Marketing operations
- Website redesigns

Keep in mind the roles. Each scrum team needs a product owner, a scrum master, and team members. The product owner for each of these scrum teams is the person who owns that functional area. If you have a marketing team this large, you may have a manager or director level person leading each of these areas. Make them the product owner.

Each team needs a scrum master, but each team does not need its own unique scrum master. You could have one person on your team be the scrum master for all of these teams. The pro of doing that is that the scrum master can focus on process and help the team get better and better. The downside, you may not have the luxury of employing a team member dedicated solely to manage process.

On the other hand, if your marketing team is this big, it might be worth the investment to have someone full-time, or nearly full-time, making sure scrum is followed and all of your teams are continuously improving. That could be worth a lot of revenue for the business. Not only will the scrum master you pick get better and better at running scrum, but your teams will continuously improve. That's a win-win.

For most teams, however, the most practical solution is to pick someone from each team to be the scrum master. Someone who is good at facilitating and who is process oriented.

Maybe the best way to start with scrum

If you are still not convinced agile marketing is right for your team, or you somehow think your team is not quite ready for full on agile marketing to replace everything you're doing, consider this small step. Pick a project type that you can run in your sleep. One that takes a few weeks to execute. Use a whiteboard and sticky notes. Don't use any technology.

For example, if webinars are something your team runs regularly, then planning your next webinar in scrum is perfect. For this reason: planning and running a webinar takes a few weeks when you consider all of the tasks from booking a guest to creating the slides to promoting the recording afterwards.

Translated.

A webinar has dozens of tasks that need to be performed over time and there are likely several milestones along the way at which you need to show some of the work to get it reviewed. Scrum works well for this. Also, pick a small team of early adopters or those on your team who are good at taking on new tasks. Pick your go-getter to do this.

Let's take some practical advice from Jeff Sutherland. He suggests the following steps to set up your first scrum project:

Pick a product owner: Who owns the webinar and makes the decisions on what webinar should be run, how, etc.

Pick a team: In this case, include the speakers, moderator, and any stakeholders.

Pick a scrum master: Pick the person who will make sure the team follows the scrum process.

Create and prioritize a product backlog: Make a list of all tasks that need to get done for the webinar. Create sticky notes and paste them on the wall in the column labeled "To Do."

Refine and estimate the product backlog: Move the sticky notes around to prioritize them.

Sprint planning: Schedule and run your first sprint planning meeting. Decide, as a team, what tasks you will get done in your first sprint.

Make work visible: Get your scrum board on the white board or wall in the office. Put all those sticky notes up on it.

Daily stand-up: Every morning for 15 minutes meet with the team and go through the three daily stand up questions. You could do these 3 days each week if you like.

Sprint review: At the end of the sprint, make the tasks done, and then share the completed tasks with any other stakeholder who needs to know the status of this webinar. Include people here who are not part of the scrum team.

Sprint retrospective: After the sprint review, run a retrospective with the scrum team to review what went well in the sprint and what did not go well and what you can do to improve during the next sprint.

If you do this for a single project, like a webinar, you will have a good feel for how scrum works. You will also gain confidence in scrum. Enough confidence that you could expand it to the rest of your team and for all other marketing projects.

Conclusion

"Think big. Start small." ~ Patricia Fripp

There can be something intimidating about adopting a new process of work. On the one hand, when you read the description of kanban or scrum, it is quite a simple process. On the other hand, there are quite a few details in the process to implement. There is the process of working in this new way, then there are the tools you need to set up. It can be intimidating. I know.

I urge you to start. Just start.

Remember back to earlier in the book where I describe how we started in agile. We started with kanban. And we didn't even implement every little part of kanban. We started with a workflow, a board, and color-coded cards. We added the swimlanes later. We have never implemented the process of limited work in progress, although I think we should.

The point is that we just started. Imperfectly. Not knowing everything about the process. We just started.

And it was great. It opened up a new way of looking at our work. We were more productive (we published on our blog more consistently). Our work was more predictable. We could visually see what work was done, almost done, in progress and if there was nothing in progress.

It was liberating.

It inspired us to move to scrum and apply it to the rest of our team's work. All of our marketing work. It did not happen all at once. We started with one small step. Mastered that small step. Then built on that. That is the secret to trying anything new. In my humble opinion.

I hope that you found in these pages, a new way of looking at your work; a roadmap for how to change your work. You know in your heart that the way our marketing teams are working today is not sustainable. There are just too many things coming at us, and we cannot keep up. We need to change everything. We need a way to prioritize our work, for real. We need a way to say "no." We need a way to focus on the highest possible contributions to our organization. I believe agile marketing is that way, and I believe you can implement it, and become the innovative marketer who you've always wanted to become.

The only things you have to do is start.

So.

Start.

Resources

Manifesto for Agile Software Development - http://agilemanifesto.org/

Agile Marketing Manifesto - http://agilemarketingmanifesto.org/

The Scrum Guide - https://www.scrum.org/resources/scrum-guide

The Death of a Marketer: Modern Marketing's Troubled Past and a New Approach to Change the Future by Andrea Fryrear

Hacking Marketing: Agile Practices to Make Marketing Smarter, Faster, and More Innovative by Scott Brinker

Scrum: Doing Twice the Work in Half the Time by Jeff Sutherland, co-creator of scrum

Scrum Marketing: Applying Agile Methodologies to Marketing by James S. Wright

Atlassian University - https://www.atlassian.com/university

ServiceRocket Atlassian Services http://atlassian.servicerocket.com

About the Author

Bill Cushard is the director of marketing and software adoption evangelist at ServiceRocket, a software adoption company, based in Palo Alto, CA, helping organizations adopt innovative software through education, implementations, support, and software applications. After observing the profound negative impact of poorly used software in organizations, Bill dedicated his career to helping organizations get the most out of their software investments. With master's degrees in both business and education, Bill approaches software projects with one eye on helping an organization achieve desired outcomes and the other eye on helping people learn the new skills necessary to thrive in an environment in which rapidly changing software drives how successful we are at our jobs.

You will notice very quickly that Bill takes a helpful approach in his writing, in his work, and on the podcasts, Helping Sells Radio and Nice Work! An Atlassian Ecosystem Podcast (iTunes, Stitcher, and maybe your other favorite podcast app).

You can connect with Bill at servicerocket.com, billcushard. com, on Twitter (@billcush), and on Linkedin (linkedin.com/in/ billcushard).

33252660R00103

Printed in Great Britain
by Amazon